Advance praise for

Sensual Faith

"Effortlessly blending scholarship and sass, *Sensual Faith* came to set the captive free. Ain't no way you can encounter what Lyvonne did in these pages and stay the same!"
    —CANDICE MARIE BENBOW, author of *Red Lip Theology*

"*Sensual Faith* is arguably controversial for those who limit their spirituality to Western traditional ideas and norms. But those seeking to ask hard questions in the pursuit of liberation will find that this book gives them permission to heal. Lyvonne's writing is a labor of love and courageous honesty. Readers will find new ways of seeing themselves in the world, free from life-limiting beliefs and equipped to thrive."
    —ROMAL TUNE, author of *Love Is an Inside Job:*
    Getting Vulnerable with God

"Lyvonne Briggs has lit a flare on the path toward boundless freedom for Black women by penning *Sensual Faith*. She gives liberatory language to our existence as 'works of art and works in progress at the same damn time.' This book holds a welcoming space for evolving spiritual and sexual identities, however expansive or particular."

—BRITTANY BROADDUS-SMITH, LSW, MEd, international Christian sexologist, founder of The Intimacy Firm, and author of the My Vulva & Me anthology series

"Lyvonne Briggs is the pastor you've always wanted—no, needed—but never dared dream existed: fearless, fabulous, and unflinchingly talking taboo. *Sensual Faith* is a ground-breaking work of spiritual decolonization and a powerful reclamation of the body."

—LINDA KAY KLEIN, author of *Pure: Inside the Evangelical Movement That Shamed a Generation of Young Women and How I Broke Free*

Sensual
Faith

Sensual Faith

The Art of Coming Home to Your Body

Lyvonne Briggs

Foreword by Briana Boyd, PhD

CONVERGENT
New York

A Convergent Books Trade Paperback Original

Copyright © 2023 by Lyvonne Briggs
Foreword by Briana Boyd, PhD, copyright © 2023 by
Penguin Random House LLC

Published in the United States by Convergent Books,
an imprint of Random House, a division of
Penguin Random House LLC, New York.

CONVERGENT BOOKS is a registered trademark
and its C colophon is a trademark of
Penguin Random House LLC.

Unless otherwise noted, all Scriptures are quoted
from the New Revised Standard Version (NRSV).

LIBRARY OF CONGRESS CATALOGING-IN-PUBLICATION DATA
Names: Briggs, Lyvonne, author.
Title: Sensual faith / Lyvonne Briggs.
Description: New York : Convergent, [2023]
Identifiers: LCCN 2022036813 (print) | LCCN 2022036814 (ebook) |
ISBN 9780593443217 (trade paperback) | ISBN 9780593443200 (ebook)
Subjects: LCSH: Sex—Religious aspects. | Body image in women—
Religious aspects. | Spiritual life.
Classification: LCC BL65.S4 B75 2023 (print) | LCC BL65.S4 (ebook) |
DDC 204/.4082—dc23/eng/20221115
LC record available at https://lccn.loc.gov/2022036813
LC ebook record available at https://lccn.loc.gov/2022036814

Printed in the United States of America
on acid-free paper

crownpublishing.com

2nd Printing

Book design by Alexis Capitini

To my grandmother
Norma Yvonne Osbourne.

You reside in my cheekbones and my will.
Thank you for guiding me from
the Great Beyond.
'Til we meet, I'll look for you at my altar
and in my reflection.

Foreword

Self-love can be an overused and thus subsequently empty term. These days, we can find countless sources of information, particularly on the internet and in social media, about the importance of loving oneself, but no in-depth information on what that tangibly means or how to arrive there. Through my own journey, I learned that self-love is a practice that must be embodied, felt, sensed. This book is a step-by-step method to effectively guide Black women/femmes back home, into their bodies, safely, and with love.

My name is Dr. Briana Boyd and I am a licensed clinical psychologist. I am a Black-white biracial woman, born and raised in Los Angeles, California, in the 1980s. I had traveled the world by the time I was twenty-one years old, and graduated cum laude with my bachelor of arts by twenty-two. I attended graduate school for my master's and doctorate and completed my PhD in clinical psychology at twenty-eight. By my early thirties I had become a trauma specialist, having treated hundreds of people, including assault survivors and combat veterans with post-traumatic stress disorder (PTSD). At the same time, I was an adjunct professor at a major university, had a thriving private practice, and worked on cutting-edge scientific research. I was retained as a consultant in forensic settings and as a subject-matter expert in PTSD, and I testified in murder and assault trials. I had achieved all my professional goals before I was thirty-five years old.

But through all these objectively impressive achievements, one thing remained consistent and true: I hated myself. I hated my body, my shortcomings, and my failures. The voice in my head blamed me for everything, and she was constantly whispering critical narratives: that others were angry at me, that everything was my fault, or that I simply was not good enough. At the time, I had no idea what self-love was, or that I didn't have it. My own self-love journey started some years ago and I'll save the full story for my own book one day, but I can say that it began with my body and the permission I started giving myself to feel safe in my own skin.

Through that process, I realized that much of my self-hatred was rooted in poor body image, which I inherited from white supremacy and misogyny, and which my mother and my mother's mothers passed on, through them, to me. I developed methods to radically decolonize the private space inside of myself and slowly began to reclaim my sense of wholeness over time. Learning to decolonize my internal space and unapologetically love myself and my God, in my ways, was my doorway to freedom, peace, grace, rage, compassion, ease, fulfillment, joy, play, sensuality, abundance, and love. Now I teach others how to do the same.

Sensual Faith would have been the perfect companion for

me on my journey in those early, unsteady years of learning to love and accept myself and my body—especially because it centers Black women/femmes. At that time there was a dearth of resources that contained information defining self-love or how to practice it. The limited resources and spaces that I did find felt very white, but I needed a book that reflected my unique journey as a biracial Black woman with the especially heavy burdens of internalized white supremacy, hyper- and hyposexualization, racism, misogynoir, and religion. *Sensual Faith* is that book. And Lyvonne Briggs reminds us that we as Black women are worthy, powerful, and right; we are God's perfect creations.

I am a therapist and, being totally honest, I was Lyvonne's therapist. (Don't worry, she signed a release of information and asked me to write about our work together in therapy for this foreword.) As a healer, I have a deep appreciation for the healers who are also on their own healing journeys. The pioneers out in front discovering the medicine, testing the medicine on their own wounds, and then carrying the medicine back from the outer realms. It takes tremendous courage and deep faith to be on—and to stay on—a healing journey. Lyvonne Briggs has that courage and faith.

I've never seen anyone work like Lyvonne has worked in therapy. Her healing process has been relatively rapid and extremely deep because she truly lets herself *feel*. She is able to sense every part of herself and every part of her experience. During our sessions, I witnessed her feeling every emotion openly and acutely, welcoming them all with courage, faith, and reverence. I have walked with her through harrowing moments in her life when she did not know which way was up or how she would move forward, facing deep, old, painful personal and family wounds, as well as collective wounds of racism, migration, religion, sexism, and colonialism. This has never stopped her from continuing to put one foot in front of the other to keep going to the edge. For her kin, for her ancestors, for her descendants, for us all. And bringing back with her *Sensual Faith,* the powerful medicine from her own healing journey. A manifesto of her own sensual journey. Her own self-love journey. Her own healing journey. Her own liberation journey. Her own journey back home.

Lyvonne is one of the most magical women I have ever met. Supporting and witnessing Lyvonne on her journey of healing, love, and spiritual expansion has been a true honor. It has also been devastating and joyous, deeply painful and exalted. There is truly no place this woman will not go inside of herself. No part of herself she is unwilling to welcome home. Lyvonne is on the journey. And there is no one better to help support you, Sis, on your journey back home to yourself and to your body.

Lyvonne is a Black body- and sex-positive Christian preacher who brings us the message that faith, sensuality, and sexuality are our birthrights. That being faithful and sexually exploratory in our own bodies are one and the same. Lyvonne is consistently willing to expand her understanding of what God and love mean. She is one of the most nonjudgmental preachers I have met to date, someone for whom doctrine truly is centered on, and deeply rooted in, love, sensuality, liberation, and womanism.

While reading *Sensual Faith,* I began to imagine how my life could have been shaped should I have had the opportunity to meet a Black body- and sex- positive Christian woman preacher when I was young. I reflected on the shame I felt in my early years about my body, which was developing much faster and fuller than the bodies of my peers, and the messages I would receive from adults in the community regarding how I, with such curves, should conduct myself. Or much older men making advances toward me and accusing me of lying about my age, or not desiring their gazes. The tone of accusation in these "helpful suggestions" and the attention to my physical appearance made me feel exposed, untrustworthy, and debauched.

This book reminds us how the presence of Black women like Lyvonne in our religious and secular communities, or resources like *Sensual Faith* in our bookstores, libraries, and churches, has the power to shape culture and discourse. The way we talk to and about Black women in their bodies matters and can effect powerful change in the lives of all Black women, from our baby girls to our wise aunties. *Sensual Faith* offers a safe, compelling, honest, and fun space to have these conversations, and Lyvonne leads them with sensitivity, strength, resolve, and integrity.

Sensual Faith is a comprehensive guide for Black women on coming home into our bodies. One of my favorite features of this book is the Reflect, Celebrate, and Affirm section at the end of each chapter. This is an invitation into practice and embodiment, elements that I historically struggled with as an academic. I appreciate how Lyvonne brings the power of practice to the information. I personally love the affirmations. I believe self-talk is one of the most important and powerful tools we can utilize to feel safe and at home in our bodies. The affirmations in this book are especially precious and powerful. I loved whispering the sweet nothings to myself and could feel myself grow in self-love and self-power every day.

I believe there is a path to self-love and internal peace for everyone. For me, it was originally through surrendering to love through the body. For some it will be through ritual. For others it might be meditation or breathing, or a recovery journey from codependency, addiction, or trauma. For some still, it may be a reclamation of faith or tradition through a womanist lens. And perhaps for many of us it will be this book, *Sensual Faith,* that will put us on our path to self-love and acceptance.

There are many among us who are standing at the precipice of greatness, of freedom, of liberation. Lyvonne has her wings wide open. In this book, she is soaring. On a personal note, Lyvonne, I could not love you more. I am beyond impressed with your healing work and what you were able to bring forth, through you, to the world. Medicine for the *bodies* and *souls* of Black women. A clear pathway home, to ourselves. I bow deeply in reverence and gratitude to you and your powerful work in therapy, and your masterpiece, *Sensual Faith.* Thank you, thank you, thank you.

Briana Boyd, PhD
Licensed Clinical Psychologist

Contents

Author's Note

Hey, boo! My name is Lyvonne, I'm originally from New York City, the daughter of Caribbean immigrants, and I am NOT your mama's preacher. I am a body- and sex-positive pastor. Gasp! Clutch your pearls! FAINT. Come to, Sis. Grab some water. It's going to be a juicy ride.

Now, you might be wondering what on Blue Ivy's green earth is a body- and sex-positive pastor? Essentially, I am a Black woman spiritual leader who is no longer at war with her body. And now, I am helping y'all to not be at war with your bodies, too! How do I do that? Well, I'm so glad you asked. I invested thousands of hours and dollars in my theological education. I have served in both sacred and secular institutions to lead some really tender conversations, a role that I certainly evolved into. When I reflect on my education, expertise, and experience, however, it's clear that, even at a young age, I knew my power was in my voice.

My mom and I used to take the subway from our Black, middle-class Queens neighborhood to the swanky, white Upper East Side of Manhattan, where she worked and I attended preschool. One morning, I felt particularly rambunctious and was asking my darling mother a slew of questions. All the while, agitated subway riders, in their varying precaffeinated states, would have much preferred that this cute but supremely chatty four-year-old would hush up. Mommy (this is her favorite part of the story, by the way) ignored the evil glares of those F-train onlookers and lovingly nudged me: "What else?"

"What else?" is an affirmation of the body, an invitation of the mind, and a celebration of the spirit. It beckons the speaker to go deeper because the hearer is truly listening. Like my mom, I am asking "What else?" to this day. While navigating the old boys' club of ministry and discerning how to be the minister that *I* needed when I was a child, I learned how to foster holistic, healthy, nuanced, multilayered conversations beyond antiquated, outdated cultural norms. The countless sermons I had heard preached about how evil women are and how our bodies must be tamed no longer fit the woman I was becoming. I knew there had to be something . . . *else*. And I know you sense that, too; otherwise, you wouldn't be holding this book, beloved.

So, I'm asking you to consider, in the words of my friend, queer theologian Xan West, "Who does it serve?" Who does it serve for you to think that your body—in all of its God-given glory—is evil? Who benefits from you believing that your body-temple is something that needs to be mastered, beaten, or lorded over? The colonized religion of our childhood made us feel like our bodies are inherently offensive to God, mere apparatuses that we need to subdue. How can we claim God is good and honor the Bible when it says: *God looked at her* Creation and declared it was* **good**,[1] yet we deem ourselves "bad"? Some bodies got some things wrong along the way!

My mother is from the island of Barbados and my father is from Guyana in South America, both former British colonies. As such, I acknowledge that, in addition to the myriad social ills in the Continental U.S., my upbringing includes fresher layers of British imperialism and colonialism. Colonizing is the very antithesis of liberating. This understanding urges me to embrace a freedom model that fully sheds the patriarchal, anti-Black, anti-woman nature of colonized religions. I reject any ideology that does not nurture my wholeness, sovereignty, and agency. The layers of westernized thinking I shed most recently gave me space to spiritually evolve and explore African Traditional Religions (ATRs).

Ghana declared 2019 "The Year of the Return" as a way to commemorate the 400th anniversary of the first enslaved Africans reaching American shores. This season of remembrance invited children of the African Diaspora to return to the Continent as a way to reconnect with our ancestral roots and heritage. Sadly, I did not journey home during that auspicious time, but I absolutely *adored* seeing all of the photos and videos on social media as travelers shared their experiences of being welcomed home by our African kin.

There is something beautiful and timeless about not being related by blood, but still being knit together as a tribe. The way we claim neighborhood kids as our play-cousins and call our women elders "Auntie" (even without any biological relation to our parents) is indicative of the tribal nature of Black folks. We are communal by design and accustomed to

---

* God is not bound by gender. God is big enough to be "her." See God as a mother hen in Matthew 23:37 and Luke 13:34.

being in and among extended communities. Our African siblings and elders were waiting to receive us, to affirm us as beloved children with a familiar home—not refugees in a strange land.

Similarly, you might be estranged from it, but your sensuality is not a stranger. You might not speak the language yet, but your sexuality is not a foreigner. They each have a home—inside of you. The REAL you. The you created in the image and likeness of God (Genesis 1:27).

In ancient West African religions, particularly the Yoruba tradition of Ifa, there is no separation between the sacred and the secular. Every . . . single . . . thing . . . is sacred. This framework creates social norms, values, and mindsets that celebrate, rather than vilify, Black/African/African-descended women's bodies. Naming and honoring that which is holy in our body-temples makes us God on the earth. We are human expressions of the Divine. We are not territory to be conquered. We are God's good Creation, meant to be cherished. Many of us are healing not only our own woundedness, but that of our foremothers as well.

It is time to come home, beloved. This is your calling card. Your ancestors are calling you. Your God is aligning with you. Your community is supporting you. The liberated woman of faith you desire to be is on the other side of your comfort zone. Now all you have to do is take a deep cleansing breath, say a quick prayer, set a loving intention, and start your journey back to your home.

If you're with me, grab a journal (the one you have stashed in the tote bag from that conference back in 2014 will suit just fine!), brew a cup of tea, and let's get into it!

One final note before we begin, beloved. This book comes with a content warning. A content warning is a statement at the start of a conversation, video, or writing that alerts the listener or viewer or reader that there are going to be some potentially distressing topics discussed.

Because I am fully aware that when I am in a room full of Black women, woundedness is present, I invite you to:

Go at your own pace.
Pay attention to feelings that come up for you.
Take breaks as you need to.
Seek support or counseling if you can.
You can do this. You can do hard things!

Go with God, beloved. . . . I'll see you on the journey.

With deep love and gratitude,
Lyvonne

Sensual
Faith

Chapter 1

Aching for Home

Learning to Ease Spiritual Homesickness

It was the day of what would have been my third wedding anniversary. Which just so happened to be the day after Mother's Day—which was already triggering for me due to a strained relationship with my mother. This was in addition to having suffered a miscarriage just five months prior. On top of that, I was searching for a new place to live because the homeowner I was renting from sold the house I was calling home. Did I mention that this all happened during a pandemic? *woozy face emoji*

GURL.

Of COURSE I was lying in my bed, crying. Weeping. Wailing. I was grieving. Depressed. Overwhelmed.

Unable to pray for myself, I texted a Sista-friend who

assured me that she was praying for me (e-ba shan-doh!), *and* she reminded me of the sage wisdom of oracle Maryam Hasnaa:

"God has the perfect home for you!"

This exclamation was just the affirmation I needed. I got up, took off yesterday's grave clothes, stripped my bed bare, changed my sheets, ran a hot bath, put a spiritual bath* on the stove, and with music and my voice, shifted the energy around myself:

God has the *perfect* home for me!

> HOME IS NOT AN ADDRESS. HOME IS WHERE YOU FEEL SAFE. AND YOUR BODY IS ACHING TO BE YOUR HOME.

Yes. The Divine had the perfect lavish, fully furnished, one-bedroom, waterfront apartment in store for me. . . . *And:*

God has the perfect home for *you*!

You see, Sis, home is not an address; home is where you feel safe.

I find God in community. So, I like to be around people with whom my soul can slouch. I don't have to pretend, perform, or put on; I can just *be*. These people are safe spaces where I find affirmation, joy, and acceptance.

But what happens when we can no longer look to other people to give us our sense of security? How do we validate ourselves from within? Where do we turn when we feel disease in our own skin?

We turn inward. We (re)turn home.

---

* A spiritual bath is a homemade elixir of various herbs, spices, and oils. Think self-baptism ritual with Esther-worthy opulence.

God Has the Perfect Home for You

Growing up in church, many of us learned that our body "is the temple of the Holy Ghost."[1] This trope compelled us to believe that we needed to be "pure" in order to prove our commitment to our faith. We equated our chastity with our worthiness as spiritual women. However, religious institutions have failed to provide Black women* with a safe space to explore our earthly body-temples. We are spiritual beings experiencing a physical existence and it's time we start acting like it.

After all, God's Self came to the earth in the form of the one we call Jesus the Christ, as a North African man and, as Rev. Dr. Mack King Carter put it, "a nigga from Nazareth."[2] With melanated hands and feet and toes and elbows. "God's love expressed in Jesus Christ means that God loves our very bodies."[3] If the Divine would manifest in Black flesh, then *surely* our flesh is good. And if Jesus was both human and divine, then he, too, was a spiritual being experiencing a physical existence. This means that Jesus prayed and fasted *and* had erections and wet dreams.

I can already hear your sharp gasps. Your mouth is agape, pulse increasing, brows furrowing.... *What is HAPPENING?* you wonder. For centuries, Black people, particularly Black women, have been raised to be antagonistic toward our bodies. And I, for one, have had enough; and, quite frankly, so has God.

---

* In this text, "women" (sometimes rendered as "womxn" or "womyn") is inclusive of Black cisgender and transgender women and femmes (a "femme" is a lesbian whose appearance and behavior are aligned with what's traditionally considered feminine or effeminate). Cisgender (or "cis") is a term for people whose gender identity matches the sex that they were assigned at birth. I am writing from my personal experiences as a Black cis heterosexual woman.

You're in a luscious body, darling one; and healthy bodies respond to stimuli. If all of your faculties are functioning properly, you can literally sense. You can see, hear, smell, taste, and touch. What a delicious gift it is to journey on this earth in a sensory temple!

Think of all the delightful scents you have smelled (fragrant flowers). The beautiful sights you have seen (hazy sunsets). The sumptuous textures you've felt (cozy cashmere). Now, think about the last time you smelled a fine-ass man's lush cologne. Or laid eyes on his plush beard. Or caressed his strong shoulders. All of these experiences are simply sensual, so why is it culturally acceptable to discuss the former, but considered crass to even mention the latter?

This narrative is long and storied, and I will guide us through the most transformative cultural moments that have shaped the status quo. We live in a hyper-sexualized yet hyper-repressed society that simultaneously stimulates and stifles our sexual urges. In one fell swoop, we are aroused by alluring images (literally *everywhere*—TV, movies, magazines, billboards) and then demonized for being sexually awakened by them. It is a lose-lose paradigm that requires a dramatic shift in thinking, an evolution of our theology (or "God-talk"), and a massive overhaul of our ethics.

For far too long, we have bifurcated our bodies from our spirits, treating them as opposites when they are, in fact, mutually beneficial conversation partners. It's time to extinguish these antiquated ideals that trace their roots all the way back to Plato. Plato asserted that the body and the spirit are completely separate entities, yet this couldn't be further from the truth. Platonic thinking is for the birds, and birds we are not. We are beautiful, gory, messy masterpieces "in this here . . . flesh."[4] It's time to stop silencing and start talking. It's time to stop shaming and start celebrating. It's time to destigmatize sex and start exalting it. Yeah, I said it. It's time to praise your flesh! Because your body is holy. Just as it is. And that's gospel.

Family, church, and society are the unholy trinity of perversion when it comes to women's bodies—particularly those of women of color and, especially, Black women. The colonial horrors of chattel slavery, the bigotry ensconced in white American "Christianity," and a pervasive anti-Black culture have demonized Black girls and Black women for millennia. So, it is no wonder that we have deeply embedded complexes when it comes to our bodies, let alone our sensuality and sexuality.

I am here to clear a path, dotted with both faith and intellect, to welcome Black women home. I am deeply committed to leading a pleasure-based movement that nudges current and formerly churched Black women (and those who support us) into righteous, sacred, holistic relationships with their bodies. In order to do this, we will **explore** the historical, sociological, political, and religious backdrops that got us here, and **restore** the theological, ethical, and practical elements that will lead us into religious reparations. Throughout these pages, I will carve out safe, protected space for you to:

1. Uncover your spirituality
2. Recover your sensuality
3. Discover your sexuality

These three critical components are a holy trinity of juiciness! And, as a multifaith womanist healer, I center the experiences of Black women in order to:

1. Retrieve ancestral wisdom
2. Reclaim sacred birthrights
3. Revive spiritual practices

Hol' Up! "Multifaith"?
Girl, Do You Believe in Jesus or Nah?

Yes. *And,* I am aware that my ancestors knew God before the colonizers brought their white-washed version of Jesus. The blond-haired, blue-eyed (sometimes brunette, brown-eyed) Jesus of my childhood is NOT the real Jesus. Jesus was a minimalist, Jewish, North African, revolutionary refugee. Jesus was Black. Accordingly, I subscribe to a Christ consciousness that commands us to:

1. Destroy systems of oppression
2. Center the most marginalized among us
3. Cocreate community for spiritual, social, and cultural nourishment

As such, I have evolved beyond evangelicalism and no longer identify as a fundamentalist. Rev. Michael Beckwith said, "A fundamentalist is afraid," and I am not fearful to interrogate my faith. In fact, a thinking Christian is a faithful Christian. I am also reclaiming my Christianity as an African Traditional Religion because Jesus was African. The Bible is, in fact, African. When we contextualize the sacred text, we must honor that race, as we know it, is a modern social construct and was not a factor when Jesus walked the earth. So, in terms of Black and white, there are NO white people in the Bible. The Bible is Blackity Black, Black, BLACK.

Whew! Ok.
So, What's a Womanist?

A womanist is a Black feminist or feminist of color. The term "womanist," coined by the illustrious writer, poet, and activist Alice Walker, made its debut in 1979. Four years later, Walker proffered an exquisite four-part definition of the term in her seminal text *In Search of Our Mothers' Gardens: Womanist Prose.*

Womanist

1. From *womanish*. (Opp. of "girlish," i.e., frivolous, irresponsible, not serious.) . . . From the black folk expression of mothers to female children, "You acting womanish," i.e., like a woman. Usually referring to outrageous, audacious, courageous or *willful* behavior. Wanting to know more and in greater depth than is considered "good" for one. Interested in grown-up doings. Acting grown up. Being grown up. Interchangeable with another black folk expression: "You trying to be grown." Responsible. In charge. *Serious.*

2. *Also:* A woman who loves other women, sexually and/or nonsexually. Appreciates and prefers women's culture, women's emotional flexibility (values tears as natural counterbalance of laughter), and women's strength. Sometimes loves individual men, sexually and/or nonsexually. Committed to survival and wholeness of entire people, male *and* female. Not a separatist, except periodically, for health. Traditionally universalist, as in: "Mama, why are we brown, pink, and yellow, and our cousins are white, beige, and black?" Ans.: "Well, you know the colored race is just like a flower garden, with every color flower represented." Traditionally capable, as in: "Mama, I'm walking to Canada and I'm taking you and a bunch of other slaves with me." Reply: "It wouldn't be the first time."

3. Loves music. Loves dance. Loves the moon. *Loves* the Spirit. Loves love and food and roundness. Loves struggle. *Loves* the Folk. Loves herself. *Regardless.*
4. Womanist is to feminist as purple is to lavender.[5]

Whoo, chile! See? Blackity Black. Every time I read through Walker's expansive eloquence, her words resonate with me in a new way. Every Black woman should print out these definitions and keep them somewhere she can see them every day. These words are like a soothing balm after a day full of aggressions at the office.* They can help calm your mind when you feel anxious on the subway, misunderstood in the classroom, or overlooked on dating apps. They speak directly to the experiences of Black women so we feel less isolated and alone.

My hope is that Black women would renounce the popular Malcolm X quotation that gets posted every time something awful happens to another Black woman. Rather than echo his tragic refrain, I am declaring: *The most respected person in America is the Black woman. The most protected person in America is the Black woman. The most nurtured person in America is the Black woman.* Black women are the most celebrated, lauded, and regarded. I am one of many crying out in the wilderness of institutional oppression to say that womanism will save us. *All* of us.

Womanism amplifies Black women's voices, perspectives, and lived experiences. Yes. *And,* womanism sees, acknowledges, affirms, respects, protects, and praises us. Womanism is the deeper shade of deliverance that can free us all, nudging us to create a liberative framework that, while centering on the freedom of Black women, is radically inclusive of the

---

* Hip-hop womanist scholar EbonyJanice Moore asserts that "there is no such thing as a '*micro*aggression'; an aggression is an aggression."

struggle for liberation for all. This is why womanists (and people who are *not* Black women, but who center womanism) can deliver us from evil.

Now, hear me—this is no social experiment. This is real life. Black girls', women's, and femmes' lives and well-being are at stake. The data has been gleaned from our heartbreak and the empirical evidence extracted from our resiliency. Our suffering, though preventable, can be repurposed. I believe we can become spiritual alchemists, turning our pain into potion and our wounds into wisdom. Womanism *is* the medicine.

> WOMANISM BLESSES US WITH A FOUNDATION UPON WHICH TO REBUILD A HOLISTIC FRAMEWORK FOR (RE)INTEGRATING OUR FULL SELVES. AS BLACK WOMEN, WE CANNOT SEPARATE OUR BLACKNESS OR OUR WOMANHOOD FROM OUR "SHOWING UPNESS" IN THE WORLD. WE ARE, IN FACT, INTERSECTIONAL BEINGS.

And while this school of thought seems magical, it is actually quite practical. Womanism blesses us with a foundation upon which to rebuild a holistic framework for (re)integrating our full selves. As Black women, we cannot separate our Blackness or our womanhood from our "showing upness" in the world. We are, in fact, intersectional beings.

Lawyer, civil rights advocate, and critical race scholar Dr. Kimberlé Crenshaw coined the term "intersectional." Intersectionality elevates the idea that we cannot separate any parts of ourselves from our identities. We are both Black and women, all the time; and we cannot privilege one of those identities over the other. And, honestly—why would we?

Despite facing burdens perpetuated by oppressors, Black women consistently rise and overcome. While living at the intersection of race, gender, class, sex, and sexuality in a racist, sexist, xenophobic society, Black women continuously dream up democratic designs. Our default frequency is liberation, so we offer salvation to the very country that attempts to disenfranchise us. The gory truth is that white women suffragettes (feminists) were not marching for Black women's right to vote in the early twentieth century. The unsavory reality is that Sistas faced sexism at the hands of our Brothas (Black liberationists) during the Civil Rights Movement of the 1960s. Despite a legacy of exclusion, Black women continually find themselves on the forefront of the lines of liberation.

As trying as taking this position may be, Black women are relentless in their pursuit of justice. In 2017, the state of Alabama elected a Democratic senator for the first time in twenty-five years when Black women buoyed Doug Jones to a win over Republican Roy Moore. Moore, who was accused of sexually abusing a fourteen-year-old girl when he was thirty-two, garnered 63% of white women's votes. Meanwhile, 98% of Black women voted for Jones[6] (the *obvious* choice). We literally stopped an entire state from electing a pedophile to political office.

While Black women have unstoppable political and organizing power, the illusion of white supremacy intoxicates white women who then swallow *our* greatest labor. In the 2016 presidential election, 47% of white women voters elected a racist, xenophobic, sexual predator to the highest office in the land. Meanwhile, 98% of Black women voters stood with *her,*[7] simply because Hillary Clinton was a more amenable type of problematic. This was by no means an ideal decision, but desperate times called for desperate measures! Four years later, bafflingly, the percentage rose to 53% of white women voters who cast ballots for "46-minus-1."[8] So much for those pink pussy hats.

These statistics crystallize why "womanist is to feminist as purple is to lavender." Black women's experiences are richer and deeper than white women's. It is historically proven that white women will consistently choose their whiteness (their "lavenderhood") over their womanhood, which is always to the extreme detriment of Black women. White women routinely benefit from white privilege *and* male privilege because of their proximity to white men—the same men that white women marry and give birth to. Feminism is insufficient as the central principle in Black women's liberation because feminism was carved out for white women and fiercely neglected Black women. Womanism is the way, the truth, and the life— our saving grace in our fight for justice and liberation.

To sustain ourselves, we must learn how to cocreate spiritual spaces and sacred texts that are logistically safe *and* radically hospitable for Black girls, women, and femmes. Hospitality is not about tolerance or presence, beloved. Radical hospitality knits Black women into the very fabric of the space. It says, "I see you. I hear you. I acknowledge you. I believe you. You are welcomed. You are appreciated. You are celebrated. You are loved." Black women's experiences must be affirmed as not just valid, but also *necessary* for creating spiritual belief systems that empower and uplift rather than repress and oppress.

A diverse range of scholars are counted in the great cloud of womanist witnesses: Rev. Dr. Jacquelyn Grant, the mother of womanist theology, and Rev. Dr. Katie Geneva Cannon, the mother of womanist ethics. Preachers, scholars,

> RADICAL HOSPITALITY KNITS BLACK WOMEN INTO THE VERY FABRIC OF THE SPACE. IT SAYS, "I SEE YOU. I HEAR YOU. I ACKNOWLEDGE YOU. I BELIEVE YOU. YOU ARE WELCOMED. YOU ARE APPRECIATED. YOU ARE CELEBRATED. YOU ARE LOVED."

educators, and thinkers I deeply admire include my forever dean Rev. Dr. Emilie M. Townes, Dr. Marcia Riggs, Rev. Dr. Kelly Brown Douglas, and Dr. Karen Baker-Fletcher, as well as Rev. Dr. Leslie D. Callahan, Rev. Dr. Maisha Handy, Rev. Dr. Renita Weems, and Rev. Dr. Wil Gafney. And it's not just my elders who are doing the work. My co-conspirators Rev. Dr. Melva Sampson, Rev. Dr. Irie Lynne Session, EbonyJanice Moore, Rev. Dr. Dominique Robinson, Rev. Melanie Jones, Rev. Dr. Neichelle Guidry, Candice Benbow, Minister Candace Simpson, Rev. Hazel M. Cherry, Rev. Porsha Williams Gates, and a whole millennial womanist remnant are taking up space in the word and in the world.

Gleaning from the works of my womanist foremothers, I integrate this notion of "sensual faith" as a framework that prods us to consider, affirm, and center the vantage points of Black women in order to revive our bodies and spirits to become more holistic beings, in Spirit and in truth.

My mother was the first person to show me sensual faith. Often unfussy, she painted her nails (Avon's Cherry Jubilee!) for church or when she wanted to take special care of herself. Adornment as self-care is a must for me; a generational ritual where *I* see me (and so does God). I never met my maternal grandmother, Norma Yvonne Osbourne, but in every photo I've ever seen of her, her hair is pressed and curled to perfection and she's wearing hats, dresses, and heels. A devout Christian, she was 5'9" and I'm 5'9.5" (even though I just say 5'10"). She gave me her cheekbones, her stature, and her faith. And it's because of them that I was able to bravely explore and embrace spirituality that feels good to *me*.

Dr. Baker-Fletcher lifts up the Bible as a primary source. And while I honor the Bible as a hallowed book of the Christian tradition, I also expand my definition of "sacred text" to include those works that capture the voices and perspectives of Black women. Using a womanist lens, a sacred text could be poetry, music, song lyrics, or even dance. Zora Neale Hurston, Toni Morrison, and Audre Lorde have all contributed to a holy literary canon that bears in its body the beauty of Black womanhood.

Movement is a sacred text. Josephine Baker, Judith Jamison, and Debbie Allen have incorporated living epistles that express Black women's deepest emotions. Poetry (Maya Angelou and Lucille Clifton), theater (Ntozake Shange and Pearl Cleage), hip-hop (Lauryn Hill and Rapsody), and film and television (Julie Dash and Ava DuVernay), all fill in the gaps gouged into our lives by patriarchal, misogynistic, misogynoirist* writings. Amplifying these artists offers us direct pathways to Black women's ways of talking, thinking, and being.

But Centering Black Women Means Decentering People Who Aren't Black Women!

Mhmm . . . that's the point.

We must liberate our minds, our faith, and our spirituality; but before we can do that, we must decolonize our bodies. A womanist lens is imperative to centering Black women's bodies. Womanist theology is critical for helping us learn what God is saying about our bodies *and* what happens to our bodies. A womanist ethic will guide us in developing practical tips and applications for embarking on (or deepening) our healing journeys. The hopeful outcome will be us reintegrating our bodies with our spirits and expressing the highest, fullest, most whole version of ourselves.

Womanism rejects all oppressive narratives and launches

---

* Black women face racialized sexism called *misogynoir*. "Misogynoir," a term coined by Black queer feminist Moya Bailey, is a blend of the words "misogyny" (the ingrained hatred of women) and "noir" (the French word for "black").

us onto a path of reunification, first and principally with ourselves, and then with one another. Womanism says:

> Your sexuality is a sacred gift.
> Your body is holy. Just as it is.
> Pleasure is your birthright.

It is time for us to incorporate this affirmation, flow, ease, and joy into our everyday lives—starting with our bodies. Our bodies are gifts. We are each our own unique expression of the Divine. We are Spirit-bearers forging ahead with the strength of our ancestors guiding us along the path. We are holy. Our spiritual belief systems should encourage us to see our bodies as temples of The One who made us and said: We. Are. GOOD.

Our flesh is HOLY. Which begs the questions: When did sex become "evil"? How did sexuality become a "demonic force"? Why did something meant to be so delectable become "distasteful"? I don't know about *your* Bible, but MY Bible says, "O taste and see that the Lord is good!"*

Taste *and* see? Yes, ma'am . . . it's in the text! These sensual imperatives are taken from the Holy Bible. Beyond procreation, pre- and extramarital sex, and the non-heterosexual sexual acts that will send us straight to hell (please catch my sarcasm), we *never* talk about sex in religious spaces. And yet, the God of the Hebrew Bible commanded us to "be fruitful and multiply."[9] Even still, sex is not just about making babies. While newborns are precious reminders of the circle of life, they are not the only reason to have sex.

All it takes is for you to have one conversation with a Sista who lives with infertility and just got *another* negative

---

* Psalm 34:8. I usually use "Eternal One" instead of "Lord" because of the oppressive language, but I love a good churchy phrase every now and again.

pregnancy test result. Or check in with your Soror who just suffered her third miscarriage. Or tap in with the rich aunties—women who are gloriously child-free and living deliciously full lives sans biological motherhood. They've surely got a story or two that might expand your understanding.

I know. This is not the opening of your typical pastor's sermon. But, as you can tell, I'm not a typical pastor. And I'm so glad God sent me to stop by here today to bring you the Good News: the Gospel According to Sensual Faith.

In 1968, Nina Simone was interviewed in New York City, and when asked what freedom meant to her, Queen Simone said, "No fear."[10] Her ferocity enlivens me. Who would we be if we didn't have any fear? What would we become if we released fear of our bodies? Fear of God? I believe we would be FREE free!

No matter where we are on the journey of acceptance, we have the freedom to explore our bodies. Our bodies are supernatural gifts from God. We are sensual beings. We are spiritual, yes, but we are having a physical experience. And, in this season, we get to liberate our minds, our bodies, and our faith.

We can never fully love God until we love our bodies. "To be unable to love our own bodies is not to know the full measure of God's love."[11] But how can you fully love your flesh if it's been demonized in your cultural community? You picked up this book because you have questions. Now is the time for you to do *your* work. Ask the hard questions. Be willing to traverse the dark and step into the light. Be brave enough to lean into discomfort. And, above all, release the need to have all the "right" answers.

It is my hope that my experience will give you a blueprint for healing and reconciliation with your body. I am, in the words of transgender rights activist Janet Mock, a "possibility model" for you, darling one. What works for me *might* work for you. What's right for you may not be right for someone else. And what's not right for someone else could be just what you need! Consider this book an on-ramp to creating a radically hospitable physical home for your blooming spirit. Perhaps you try everything on for size and see what fits. Or maybe you take some time to discern what feels good and right and pleasurable for you and go with your favorite choices. No matter your taste in decor, I invite you to take a deep dive into my stories and insights. Whatever your final selections, I am delighted to see how you furnish your spiritual home!

So, let's learn and explore. Let's have fun. Let's smile in the face of adversity. Laugh in the face of oppression. Love our bodies in the face of eurocentric beauty standards. Let's pleasure ourselves in place of religious sexual shame.

Remember: Home is not an address. Home is where you feel safe. And your body is aching to be your home. So that no matter where you go, you feel affirmed, nourished, and loved. But that can only happen when you decide to embrace *all* of who you are. If that sounds life-giving to you, let's journey through this *together*.

Reflect:

So God created humankind in his image, in the image of God he created them; male and female he created them. (Genesis 1:27)

Celebrate:

Trust the divine timing of your life. You are reading this book and pondering these thoughts, in *this* season, for a reason. Take some time to set intentions for this journey. Grab your journal, get quiet, and go inward.

In what ways do you want to heal your relationship to your body? How do you need God to show up in guiding you home to your body-temple? What questions have you always wanted to ask your pastor about your body, but didn't think that you could? Write for at least five minutes and see what comes up for you.

Affirm:

I am created in the image and likeness of God.
God is big enough for my questions.
Home is not an address. . . . Home is where I feel safe.

Chapter 2

"Body" Is Not a Four-Letter Word

Renewing Your Mind About Your Flesh

It was a typical Sunday night in the Briggs household and my family and I were watching *The Simpsons* together. We lounged in the living room, eight-year-old me sitting cross-legged on the large black-and-cream area rug in the center of the floor. As the animated comedy came to a close and the end credits started to roll, I could hear Homer and Marge Simpson making kissing noises. The lingering black screen, punctuated by their sensual sounds, insinuated that they were going to have sex, and my third-grade self was not here for the shenanigans.

"Ewww! That's *nasty*!" I exclaimed.

"What's nasty?" my mother lovingly inquired.

"They're about to *do it*."

"Do what?"

"It!"

I couldn't bring myself to say the word, the idea of sex held so much fear for me. My mother was both unbothered and intrigued. She wanted me to say "sex" out loud, but it held so much power, weight, and terror over me that it felt impossible to simply speak it. She wouldn't let up. "Say it. It's not nasty, it's natural. . . . Say it!"

I sobbed. I bawled. I wailed! Our struggle moved to the bathroom, where I stared at my tear-streaked cheeks in the mirror for thirty entire minutes, sniffling and refusing to say the word.

Finally, out of sheer weariness and desperation, I muttered it softly, "Sex."

"Say it again," my mother insisted.

This time, I spoke a touch louder, "Sex!"

And that was it. My mother ended the conversation, satisfied with her teachable moment. I washed my face, brushed my teeth, and went to bed. We did not discuss why I had such a hard time saying the word "sex." I do not recall ever having a holistic conversation with my parents, educators, or caregivers around bodies, sex, and intimacy. I *do* remember once taunting my brother that he would grow up to be gay (which I now know was an awful, *evil* thing to do). But my mom simply replied, "And?? So what if he is? We will love him no matter what." So, my mom did model radical inclusion of sexual orientation for me when I was in middle school; but the actual expression of said sexuality? Not so much.

If you're like me, you never heard "God," "love," and "flesh" in the same sentence. Growing up, I did not hear any sermons about our bodies. I saw my Episcopal priest enrobed from head to toe in his layered garb, and, when I became an acolyte (altar servant), I adopted my own full-body coverings. It was apparent to me at an early age that the church was *not* a place for body-talk.

I am not an anomaly. Many Black communities have done a terrible job fostering intergenerational, theologically sound, ethically responsible, and culturally whole conversations about sex and sexuality. Black religious spaces, in particular, have a void around this topic. Most Black Christians have been indoctrinated to bifurcate their bodies and their spirits, and have a tendency to use the Bible as a sort of twisted security blanket to support these antiquated ideologies.

According to The Eve Appeal, a UK charity that raises funds for gynecological cancer research, nearly half of women polled could not locate their vaginas. Just over 60% "were unsure where the vulva is," and only 30% could name all six parts (that would be the vulva, vagina, uterus, both fallopian tubes, and ovaries) correctly.[1] Most grown women do not even know what their own personal vaginas look like! That means as little girls, teenagers, or young adults, they likely did not know what their bodies looked like, either.

It is asinine that society would uphold social structures just to make Black women feel estranged from our bodies. People use eurocentric beauty ideals to make us feel unattractive and they perpetuate stereotypes about Black-girl culture to caricaturize us. Familial obligations drain our time and life force under the guise of "giving back." I'd rather see all of the energy we spend on learning how to love ourselves in an anti-Black, anti-woman world instead be used for deep spiritual transformation to create a world where Black women are celebrated, lauded, and regarded. But radical self-love is seen as revolutionary and that is infuriating. Why is it countercultural for me to love myself the way God made me?

In a word: capitalism. Feeling at home in your body requires due diligence because there is a four-billion-dollar "beauty" industry whose sole purpose is to destroy your sense of value and self-worth. As a tall, dark-skinned, bald, blond (for now!) baddie with hips, thighs, cellulite, and stretch marks, I cannot wait around for affirmation from the very social structure that was designed to destroy me. Like our glorious elder, poet, activist, and educator Nikki Giovanni, said, "You don't have the right answers because you're asking the wrong people. You're asking somebody who hates you, 'Are you pretty?' What kind of sense does that make?"[2] This is the core of our joy: to heal, transform, and radically embrace the truest, purest forms of our highest selves.

I call this my Lavish Love Framework. "Lavish" as an adjective means "opulent, luxurious, or extravagant." But "lavish" is also a verb. I use it to mean we should bestow, expend, and pour out our love, and that love should start with us. Our self-love should be opulent. We should feel extravagantly well loved by ourselves. In order to radically love ourselves, we have to luxuriate in who we are. And in order to *truly* accept ourselves, we have to change our narrative. We must transform our inner dialogue to a sweet, nurturing salve that will soothe our pains, trauma, and disbeliefs. Acknowledging, believing, and understanding that our bodies are good (not bad), sacred (not secular), holy (not evil), requires a rewiring of our spiritual, theological, and moral compass.

If you grew up hearing harmful messaging from the pulpit, like these, you were done a great disservice by your spiritual leadership:

> THIS IS THE CORE OF OUR JOY: TO HEAL, TRANSFORM, AND RADICALLY EMBRACE THE TRUEST, PUREST FORMS OF OUR HIGHEST SELVES.

If you have sex before marriage, you're going to hell.
Keep your legs closed or else.
Good girls don't give head.

The church's "antidote" of heterosexual marriage does not undo decades of suppressive theology. Maybe you were raised in a Black Christian church: Baptist with a whooping preacher and a magnificent choir, Episcopalian with *all* the frankincense and myrrh, or nondenominational with flannel shirts and fog machines. Even if you no longer attend church or were never particularly religious to begin with, the church has affected your life, because the church has deeply impacted cultural norms and conditioning.

It's like when in the movie *The Devil Wears Prada,* the main character, Andy, snickers about her fashion team's indecision to choose from two similar but different blue belts. The villain, Miranda, in no friendly terms, informs Andy, essentially: *You don't think you're being affected by fashion, but the people in this very room chose it for you.* You can say you are spiritual but not religious, but you cannot deny that you are affected by puritanical religious ideals.

The Black Church was birthed out of our ancestors' desire to worship their God in a safe, protected space away from their white terrorist counterparts. Over recent centuries, however, the Black Church has morphed into a hollowed-out version of its former sanctuary-self. The liberation of our people has been decentralized by internalized oppression and unethical practices. Where once we were God's people, now we are not people at all.* We are just membership numbers. Tithes. Offerings. Giving campaigns. Building funds. Fish fries. Chicken dinners.

That is not to say that *every* predominantly Black Christian church is dysfunctional. There is, after all, a critical mass of pastors, preachers, teachers, ministers, lay leaders, and congregants who are committed to the liberation of *all* Black people: Black women, femmes, trans folx, queer folx, men,

---

* An inversion of 1 Peter 2:10.

children, and non-gender-conforming peeps. *E'rybody*. Every *body*. And, as a Black, straight, cisgender woman, I am aware of the great privilege that I have even as I inhabit multiple marginalized identities. I honor that every ethical path that does not cause harm is valid. I also hold space for those of us who heard harmful messaging, either from the pulpit or our parents.

When You Got That Flow

Sleeping with an overnight pad should be categorized as an Olympic sport. Those of us with functioning female reproductive organs know all too well the morning game of "Did I or didn't I?" when it comes to spotting on your clothes or bedsheets. When I was a teenager, I used tampons during the day to soak up the outpouring of blood, but at bedtime my period required heavy-duty apparatuses—namely, twin extra-long overnight pads that felt more like menstrual diapers.

One cycle, my flow missed my pad and bled onto my underwear. I took my stained undergarment into the bathroom with me, planning to handwash it while I was in the shower. However, I forgot about it and accidentally left it hanging on the shower curtain rod. About ten minutes later, I heard my father shouting my name.

"Lyvonne!"

"Yes?"

"Come here!"

When I poked my head around the corner, I saw my father pointing at my blood-stained banner.

"Move these. . . . That's disgusting. Your brother and I shouldn't have to see that!"

My father was offended by the mere presence of my bloodied underwear. It's not like I had it framed and displayed as protest art. I simply had forgotten to launder it and bring it out of the bathroom with me! I was irritated by my father's behavior, but I apologized anyway.

Interactions like the one between my father and me show how Black girls learn to internalize negative messaging about themselves and their bodies. Here was an opportunity for my parent to offer grace and affirmation for a truly natural occurrence, but instead, his harsh language and disgusted tone ended up making me feel like I had to defend my body and protect myself.

How could something as commonplace as a menstrual cycle be seen as "bad"? It's because men do not have menstrual cycles. And, thanks to the patriarchy, the feminine figure has been demonized for millennia, even (especially!) in the Bible. Abraham's wife, Sarah, was vilified for her beauty; Lot's wife was turned into a pillar of salt for simply looking back; and Job's wife was stereotyped as an infidel when, in her grief, she shouted, "Why don't you just curse God and die!"[3] And that's just a small portion of the Old Testament!

In Sunday school, we learned that Eve ate the apple and caused the fall of humanity, and her sinfulness is why we suffer menstrual cramps and childbirth pain. WOW. There are thousands of medical service providers who would affirm that muscle contractions are what actually cause labor pains. Women have been living with these aches since the beginning of time, before the Bible was written, let alone published, and male religious leaders decided that *that's* the explanation we're rolling with? Ok, sir. *eyeroll*

According to the Torah, a woman who has her period is ritually "unclean." The men who wrote the Bible labeled menstruating women as "dirty." They were not just socially distanced—they were placed in solitary confinement because of what their bodies did naturally. It still boggles my mind how male scribes couldn't revere how menstrual cycles were literally responsible for their existence on this earth! No human being would be alive were it not for women's menstrual cycles. Perhaps those ancient Brothas *knew* our power, but somewhere along the line, oppressors did what they needed to do to co-opt the text.

In biblical literature, women are shamed for being barren *and* for having a cycle. In today's culture, women are shamed for becoming mothers "too young" or "too old," for staying at home or going back to work "too soon." It's *exhausting*. And it doesn't need to be. If our bodies are healthy and functioning, they have the capacity to give life. Aside from love, life is the most powerful force on the planet. Our menstrual cycles are a beautiful representation of the life-giving nature of our godly bodies.

But we wouldn't know that from the way family, church, and society have formed misshapen language and discourse around our bodies. You don't have a "hoo-ha" or a "va-jay-jay," Sis. You have a vagina. If we are going to get to a place where we normalize conversations about our bodies, then we must consistently use the anatomically correct names for our body parts. Correctly naming our body parts is an act of spiritual reclamation. It elevates and integrates our whole selves. When we normalize conversations about our body parts, we normalize conversations about what happens to our body parts.

Because—trust me—if we're not talking about breasts and vaginas, we're also not talking about periods, regular (or irregular!) menstrual cycles, prostates, fibroids, sexually transmitted diseases and infections, unplanned pregnancies, abortion or pregnancy termination, miscarriage or pregnancy loss, sexual harm, and intimate-partner violence. Not talking about sex means not talking about the body, and that's really, *really* dangerous.

We must deconstruct any system that feeds off our bodily insecurity. In Black religious spaces, women are often shamed for our bodily functions—which is wild to me, because Christians use such body-centric language. We refer to other Christians and fellow church members as the Body of Christ. How is it culturally acceptable to be the hands, eyes, ears, and feet of Christ, but not his pinkies, hair, or ankles? As much as Christians espouse the dual nature of Christ—simultaneously divine *and* human—we lean into the puritanical ideals of an otherworldly religious figure while conveniently denying his earthly human aspects.

Jesus came to this earth in a very particular body with melanated skin. In the words of professor and priest Kelly Brown Douglas, "Jesus Christ clearly signifies that God loves us not in spite of or apart from our bodies, but that God loves us in our bodies as uniquely embodied creatures."[4]

Whether his kinky curls were styled in luscious locs or a haloed-out afro, he came as a Black *man*. That means that he had a penis, an anus, and pubic hair; just like he had elbows, nipples, and a thick, luscious beard. And, Sis . . . you know how much we love a thick, luscious beard!

Moreover, the literal body of Christ germinated inside the womb of a thirteen-year-old Black girl who, according to the biblical narrative, consented to impregnation by the Holy Spirit. So, biologically, a man had nothing to do with the incarnation and birth of Christ. The blood of Jesus is actually the blood of Mary, and so, we have a Black woman to thank for salvation.

Now, before you toss my book into the Goodwill bag for being sacrilegious, you should know that whenever you see the word "salvation" in the Bible, it means "healing." Without Mary's virgin womb, would we even be talking about healing in the Christian tradition? We should be talking about Mary's womb as much as we're talking about Jesus' body. The minimizing of Mary's womb is parallel to the erasure of Black women's bodies in the biblical text. Since writers, curators, and translators of the Bible tried to eliminate mentioning women's body parts from the Bible, it's no wonder people who believe in the Bible have tried to blot out our bodies as a whole!

It is the external mistreatment of our temples that convinces us that we need to internally dissociate from our bodies. My father's indictment of me during Bloodgate did not occur in a vacuum. Throughout his own lifetime, social structures persuaded him that women's blood was repulsive. Just look at the pseudonyms we use for our menstrual cycles: *Monthly visitor. Aunt Flo. That time of the month.* We really do try to jazz up anything that has to do with female human body parts and their functions, don't we?

It's not our fault, beloved. We have been socialized to believe that we cannot be open and honest about our natural occurrences. Women are the only people who can bleed for three to five days (or more!) straight (from our vaginas, no less) and are expected to go about our life as if it's business as usual. And those of us who are wise enough to listen to our body, slow down, and rest are called "weak" for taking downtime. If people can sympathize with LeBron James when he cramps up during an NBA Finals game, then SURELY they can learn to sympathize with women who are experiencing pain (on a MONTHLY basis) that rivals the pain caused by a heart attack.[5]

Reclaiming Autonomy

For those of us who were raised within a merit-based worthiness system, we were deemed valuable only as long as we were achieving, producing, or succeeding. We were taught that if we did not serve or please people, we would not receive love. We believed that only our hyper-achievement made us worthy of acceptance. This individualized pressure leads to hyper-productivity in Black women. In *Sisters in the Wilderness: The Challenge of Womanist God-Talk,* Delores S. Williams identifies that Black women's bodies have always been tied to production. Our enslaved foremothers were forced to procreate because any children they had were considered more property, and thus income, for enslavers. Subsequently, in this country, Black women have a history of being appraised for their labor. The residual effects of chattel slavery continue to trickle down into our interactions today.

We are not businesses. We are not profits. We are people; people who have, disturbingly, inherited a legacy of capitalism that deceives us into thinking that our worthiness is inextricably linked to our productivity. Let me remind you, beloved ones. You are *inherently* worthy. Worthy is not something you *do*. Worthy is something you *are*. You are not your business. You are not your busyness. You are a human being. And now is the perfect time to get back to being, for *being* is enough.

If you happen to struggle with feelings of unworthiness, know that you are not to blame. We live in a society that categorizes and hierarchizes people based on race, class, gender, sexuality, and status. And while we are taking the right steps to transform biases into blessings, we still have work to do with reclaiming our bodily autonomy. Williams asserts that womanist theology is exactly what we need to see God and ourselves more fully:

> Womanist theology is a prophetic voice concerned about the well-being of the entire African American community, male and female, adults and children. Womanist theology attempts to help black women see, affirm, and have confidence in the importance of their experience and faith in the African American community. Womanist theology challenges all oppressive forces impeding black women's struggle for

survival and for the development of a positive, productive quality of life conducive to women's and the family's freedom and well-being. Womanist theology opposes all oppression based on race, sex, class, sexual preference, physical ability, and caste.[6]

We were not created to serve capitalism. Our bodies are not entities outside of ourselves that we need to "beat into submission" or "die to daily." Our body-temples are divinely designed to restore themselves, but we must rest in order to do so. For rest is not a reward . . . it is our birthright. And rest helps us to indulge in soft sacred spaces where we are reminded that we are intrinsically worthy of love, concern, care, and *pleasure*. When we awaken to pleasure, then (and only then) can we show up fully in our body-temples.

How Sensuality Evolves One's View of Self

One online dictionary defines sensuality as "unrestrained indulgence in sensual pleasure," "lewdness," and "unchastity." I define sensuality as "the mindful practice of being aware of your present experiences." Sensuality is the ultimate practice of mindfulness. Being present in our bodies invites us to get grounded and curious. While we may not have been alive during ancient biblical days, we are alive now, and our bodies are living epistles: moving, breathing, growing sacred texts that proffer insight into our deep, transformational, healing journeys.

Womanist ethicist Rev. Dr. Katie Geneva Cannon discusses the importance of retrieving Black women's literary traditions for the purpose of uncovering the values by which Black women lived with moral courage in the context of racist, sexist, and gender oppression. In *Katie's Canon: Womanism and the Soul of the Black Community,* Cannon argues that "Black women are taught what is to be endured and how to endure the harsh, cruel, inhumane exigencies of life."[7]

I call this lived condition *moortyrdom*. "Moortyrdom" is a blend of "martyrdom" (suffering—even unto death, for a presumably noble cause) and "moor" (a northwestern African Muslim ethnic group; for all intents and purposes— African-descended/Black). Black women have continuously sacrificed themselves for the greater "good." Anything that celebrates and honors Black women's bodies is anti-moortyrdom. Thanks to a rising consciousness around culture and ethnic heritage, as well as an increase in digital platforms that creatives use to display stunning images of diverse women, there is a global rise in amplifying Afrocentric beauty. Eurocentric standards of beauty are being obliterated, and that is offering a whole generation of Black girls the beautiful gifts of being seen and affirmed. I'm thinking of sonic love letters like *Sesame Street*'s "I Love My Hair" and Beyoncé's "Brown Skin Girl," artistic offerings that celebrate our most precious minis from their earliest moments.

I'm a Grown Woman

People may think that I am a body- and sex-positive pastor just because I want to have sex. First, I don't need to be a body- and sex-positive pastor to want to have sex. Embracing my sexuality makes me human, not a ho.* Second, I *do* want to have extremely pleasurable, healthy, consensual, mind-blowing, life-giving sex. Third, you can't jump to sex-positive without first being body-positive. And that's where most of us have been stuck . . . until now!

---

* There's nothing wrong with being a ho, either. We don't do slut-shaming over here. Just be ethical about your "ish."

Now is the perfect time to honor that your body is holy. Sacred. *Good.* . . . Just as it is!

Reflect:

The Lord, your God, is in your midst, a warrior who gives victory; he will rejoice over you with gladness, he will renew you in his love; he will exult over you with loud singing! (Zephaniah 3:17)

Celebrate:

After taking a shower or bath, moisturize yourself from head to toe with lotion, oil, or cream (and take the time to really appreciate each nook and cranny). Maybe even kiss or say (or sing!) "I love you" to each body part. This will help you to really *see* your body as tender and sacred, even in simple everyday life.

Affirm:

I was born worthy.
I am worthy just by being.
I am enough.

Chapter 3

"I Had a Feeling"

Trusting Your Gut and Nurturing Your Intuition

*Something **told** me that was going to happen.*

Chris was handsome, stylish, quiet, and sweet. The seemingly perfect complementary blend for my exquisite, statuesque, loud, extroverted self. Plus, he could sing his behind off! Knowing that opposites attract, my best friend, Shaun, played matchmaker and set Chris and me up.

We'd made plans to connect one evening, so I used the afternoon to run some errands I had been putting off. It was wintertime, so while I was in a drugstore searching for some Emergen-C to boost my immune system (this was WAY before COVID-19), my eyes landed on Mucinex. Immediately, those commercials with the animated green orbs popped into my mind.

"Get it." I sensed an inner urge to buy it.

Mucinex? I questioned myself. *I don't need Mucinex. I don't even USE Mucinex!*

I felt a stronger urge, but shrugged it off as no big deal, grabbed a box of the Super Orange packets I originally came for, and went about my business.

Later that day, I called Chris to check in and he sounded congested.

"Oh, no! You sound terrible," I empathized.

"I know. I'll be ok. . . . I just need to buy some Mucinex," he relayed.

My mouth about hit the floor.

"It was for YOU!" I exclaimed.

"What?"

"Something told me to get some Mucinex earlier and I didn't know why, but it was for you!"

Too bad his tablets were still in the pharmaceutical aisle in the drugstore right where I'd left them!

How many times have you experienced this? You have a seemingly meaningless thought fly right by you, only to have a full-circle moment of realization later that the "passing thought" was really a premonition—a mental admonition alerting you to a pending situation. Some people call this a "gut feeling" or the Holy Spirit. That intrinsic sensing, knowing, and leading is your *intuition*.

Your intuition is a gifted guide who speaks to you from the Great Beyond. Whether it is ancestral wisdom bubbling up or a clear indication from Spirit that you are on the right path, your intuition is an embedded compass that gently nudges you in the right directions. Your intuition is a gift. She is not an exclusive benefit that you need to earn, she is an innate adviser that you get to nurture.

Most of us associate our intuition with danger. If you're walking home by yourself late at night, you trust that your survival instincts will kick into high gear if a suspicious stranger starts to follow you. That, darling one, is actually fright and survival mode. Or, say you go on a date with a new guy and you text your friends his name and license plate number so that someone knows who you were last with: That is not necessarily a manifestation of your intuition. That is a safety precaution in a world where gender-based violence, even on dates, is a very real threat. Enduring such traumatizing circumstances has a profound effect on our intuition. She has been so malnourished by our trauma and social conditioning that we do not allow her to shine in her full function. While our intuition can certainly be a signal that warns us when something is "off," it can also prod us to prepare for the future.

From the moment I saw the campus-wide email announcing that an NBCUniversal representative was coming to Seton Hall to recruit for the NBC Page Program, I got butterflies in my stomach. I didn't care what time the rep would be there, which class I had to miss, I just *knew* I had to attend the recruiter's presentation. After her slideshow and pitch, I introduced myself to her and we built a great rapport. That positive encounter led me to an interview, which led me to working as an NBC page. As a page I contacted a senior producer at NBC Olympics, which led to me being a part of an Emmy Award–winning production team for the 2008 Beijing Games for NBC Olympics. While producing a piece for NBC Olympics, I conducted research at the Yale Divinity School Library . . . which led me to apply to and matriculate at Yale Divinity School. Two advanced degrees later, I am now a spiritual leader in the public square and leading conversations on pleasure as a body- and sex-positive theologian, author, speaker, and creator. The relationships I formed at NBC have led to other personal and professional gains, and my life would not be the same without them!

. . . .

Intuition Is a Gift

If you're not sure how to follow your intuition, well, you're right *and* wrong. Chill with the side-eye, Sis, and let me explain. There's no right *or* wrong way to follow your intuition. Everyone is different—every *one* is different. The key is to distill your voice into a note that is so pure, you can trace it even in a cacophony of chaotic sounds. The way you harbor harmony is to practice listening to yourself.

Intuition is one of the highest forms of self-expression. She is the core of communication and a direct reflection of your interior life—what you think, feel, sense, and *know* without "knowing." Your "inher"* guide directs you with internal inspiration. The beauty of understanding this gift is that you do not have to *do* anything to access it. From the time God knits us together in our mothers' wombs, we are ordained worthy enough to access each of our divine gifts.

There are, however, blockages to our ability to tap into our intuition. Family, church, and society have truncated the connections between our bodies and our spirits, thus disconnecting us from the inner sanctum of our beings. Your very existence is a divine symbol of peak Intelligent Design, which orchestrated your intuition to be a very present help—both in and beyond times of trouble.

Black families, tortured by generations of anti-Black terrorism, have been groomed to be hyper-focused on trouble. Bearing about in

> YOUR VERY EXISTENCE IS A DIVINE SYMBOL OF PEAK INTELLIGENT DESIGN, WHICH ORCHESTRATED YOUR INTUITION TO BE A VERY PRESENT HELP— BOTH IN AND BEYOND TIMES OF TROUBLE.

---

* This rendering of "inner" as a compound of "in" and "her" is a reflection of the inherent feminine nature of intuition.

our bodies are the residual effects of chattel slavery, the remnants of Jim Crow, and the aggressions of modern-day racism. So much so that our pain and trauma have deeply impacted our ability to connect with our inner knowing. Internationally renowned researcher, author, educator, and speaker Dr. Joy DeGruy offers us some insight into the effects of multigenerational trauma. In her book, *Post Traumatic Slave Syndrome: America's Legacy of Enduring Injury and Healing,* DeGruy explicates that trauma has been passed down to us intergenerationally. The fancy word for this trail of tears is "epigenetics." DeGruy illuminates: "'Post Traumatic Slave Syndrome' is a condition that exists when a population has experienced multigenerational trauma resulting from centuries of slavery and continues to experience oppression and institutionalized racism today."[1]

Over time, the descendants of enslaved Africans have adapted in order to survive, both in ways that support us and demonstrate our resiliency, and in ways that no longer serve us. Rather than ignoring those harmful stories we must shift to evolve beyond outdated narratives, habits, and beliefs. Westernized, oppressive colonizers did all that they could to separate us from our African heritage, customs, and practices. Assimilation, one of the greatest scams ever, lulls us into a false sense of security by enticing us to believe that minimizing our Blackness means we will magically be accepted by anti-Black structures. In actuality, we are called to get deeply in tune with our ancestral wisdom and the ancient ways of being that lie within us.

Since Creation, we have been called to be more spiritual, holy, and godlike. Being more like God means being your authentic, divinely designed self. Living from the fullness of who you are is the greatest expression of faith. It shows that you are in direct agreement and alignment with who the Creator fashioned you to be. That's why it's critical that we do the deep inner work to heal from the rhetoric and conditioning that compels us to disregard—even hate—who we are. As Black women, we are daughters of the African Diaspora and we are entitled to her fruit.

We have African privilege.

It is our birthright to connect with the spiritual modalities of our ancestors, who, like us, were gifted with intuition and clairsentience. For those of us who grew up in conservative Black Christian households, it may take repeated reminders for us to accept that it is ok to trust our gut over our intellect. DeGruy opines:

> LIVING FROM THE FULLNESS OF WHO YOU ARE IS THE GREATEST EXPRESSION OF FAITH. IT SHOWS THAT YOU ARE IN DIRECT AGREEMENT AND ALIGNMENT WITH WHO THE CREATOR FASHIONED YOU TO BE.

"We come to understand our world through many means. We use reasoning, observation and calculation. We use our five senses and our intuition. We use symbolic imagery through stories and analogies. We use all of these and more. In order to more fully understand ourselves we need to be aware of how each of these is emphasized in African culture."[2]

Now is your divinely timed season, even if you're afraid, to tap into the "and more-ness" of your faith. Perhaps God blessed you to see visions or dream dreams or hear voices. Western psychology has not traditionally given room for supernatural prowess. But God is calling you to face any oppressive doctrine that is blocking you from tuning in to your divine gifts. In the words of Rev. Dr. Melva Sampson, "Do it scared!"

....

Intention Is the Key to Intuition

It sounds simple—just "do it scared!" But, beloved, it will take intentionality. And that is what Goddess Lulabelle encouraged us to do: "Nothing without intention. Do nothing without intention."[3] Intention setting is a lot like making a prayer request. It is a process that invites us to introspect and discover what our true desires are. Our core desires are not what our parents raised us to think we want, and they are certainly not what society tricks us into believing we should want. Our deepest, truest, most joyful core desires fully and authentically honor the passions and pursuits that bring us unspeakable joy.

In *Women Who Run with the Wolves: Myths and Stories of the Wild Woman Archetype,* Clarissa Pinkola Estés, PhD, invites us to get curious about our core desires:

> When we are connected to the instinctual self, to the *soul* of the feminine which is natural and wild, then instead of looking over whatever happens to be on display, we say to ourselves, "What am I hungry for?" Without looking at anything outwardly, we venture inward, and ask, "What do I long for? What do I wish for now?" Alternate phrases are "What do I crave? What do I desire? For what do I yearn?" And the answer usually arrives rapidly: "Oh, I think I want . . . you know what would be really good, is some this or that . . . ah yes, that's what I really want."[4]

What do you have a taste for, Sis?

Whether it is selecting a side dish for your dinner entrée or even simply choosing a restaurant to go to, we can have a hard time identifying, honoring, and prioritizing our desires. We have been raised with the belief that we must put everyone and their mama's needs before our own, thus minimizing our capacity to receive. Our minds are often cluttered with others' voices. We need to "Marie Kondo" our interior lives in order to discard the thoughts that no longer serve us, cultivate the ideas that need a bit more fleshing out, and embrace the new mantras that will strengthen us for the journey. In this moment, you may not know what the "right" way is. But if you are gracious with yourself and begin to heed those gentle, loving nudges, you will eventually become so in tune with your inner guidance that you will find it hard to recall a time when you didn't.

First, though, we must actively unclog the emotional drains that are impeding our flow. Many of us learned early on that our survival depended on our silence, so we quieted the voice that told us "this is wrong" or "speak up." Our cultural context added to our harbored hushes. We were raised hearing that "children are to be seen and not heard"—rhetoric that is completely asinine! Children are the closest we *get* to God! They are fresh from the ancestral plane and come bearing piping-hot spiritual tea; but because of some of our terrifying intergenerational upbringings, we do not honor the agency of our children.

From a young age, we as Black, female children were hyper-sexualized and treated as if we were older than we actually were. A study on the adultification of Black girls conducted by Georgetown Law's Center on Poverty and Inequality found that adults viewed Black girls as young as five (5!) as needing "less nurturing, protection, support, and comfort than white girls of the same age."[5] With teachers, pastors, coaches, and other caregivers believing these falsehoods, it's no wonder our childhoods were like vapor in the wind. We spent our tender years dodging racists, sexists, *and* pedophiles. That's not what childhood is supposed to be about. Some of us are blaming ourselves for things that simply weren't our fault. And if we cannot forgive ourselves for something we didn't do, we end up perpetually stuck. Additionally, the religion of our girlhood taught us that we were "shapen in iniquity" and born into "sin."[6] How do you believe in yourself when you are constantly told that you were vile from conception? We must renounce the narrative that tells us that we are inherently evil. We are *not* inherently evil. We are intrinsically good. We are holy. We are loved.

Who would you be if you had heard *those* words throughout your childhood?

Ultimately, we heal our intuition by healing our inner child. Our inner child is the baby girl living inside of us, who is craving attention after being neglected and desires to be heard after being silenced. How can you feel at home in a space that was taken from you at a young age? Many of us are forever changed from what researchers call Adverse Childhood Experiences (ACEs for short). Dr. Nadine Burke Harris, author of *The Deepest Well: Healing the Long-Term Effects of Childhood Adversity,* asserts, "We are all affected by ACEs in similar ways." What happens in your childhood shows up in your adult years and "many people who have experienced ACEs and are grappling with their lifelong effects don't know what they are dealing with."[7]

Why talk about my inner child? you ponder. *I'm a grown woman!* That may be true, darling one, but you are also a woman who has experienced woundedness. It is no wonder that you are still learning how to trust yourself, as you have not been listening to the most precious voice you know— your little you. The core of our transformation lies in the ways that we nurture our inner children, which is also known as "reparenting."

What did you need but not get as a child? What didn't Mommy say? What didn't Daddy do? And how are these gaps showing up in your life today? I know as an adult it's tempting to focus on your to-do list, but try to remind yourself that you *are* your first to-do. Pause for a moment to take a deep breath and assess your needs; pamper, nurture, cherish, and nourish yourself. Don't be afraid to tell yourself what you need to hear in order to feel and be ok. Grab your journal and write a letter to yourself. Stand in front of the mirror and speak to your reflection. In every way, offer yourself the compassion that was withheld from you but you so richly deserve.

It is particularly key that we heal our Mommy wounds.* Intuition is an inherently divine feminine trait, and a lot of the barriers to accessing her are due to mothering wounds. Like sacred, divine, feminine energy, inner-child work is intrinsically intuitive. When you pay attention to the desires of the little girl inside of you, you are listening to the soul of who you are. Above and beyond that, you are inviting the most pure version of yourself to come alive. The You *before* the labels, boxes, and classifications. The You *before* the trauma, abuse, and social conditioning.

This is why it is critical for us to heal beyond an American, white terrorist "Christianity" that demonizes Blackness and womanhood, and evolve to an African-centered spiritual system that radically embraces and celebrates all of God's Creation. In ancient West African spirituality, one needs both masculine *and* feminine energy in order to be complete. In most Christian churches (Black, white, or multiracial), the Divine Feminine is minimized, devalued, and diminished. Black sacred spaces, in particular, are often steeped in patriarchal, sexist, misogynistic, misogynoirist rhetoric that represses, suppresses, and oppresses women and sacred

---

* Jennifer Arnise is a fabulous resource. She is the premier expert on healing the Black mother wound so we can, in her words, "stop being so damn strong and start accessing the transformative power of vulnerability and tenderness."

feminine energy. This subjugation is tragic because divine feminine energy is a complement to divine masculine energy.*

Logical, linear thinking is an inherently masculine trait, which is why in westernized, patriarchal societies, data is king. Science requires consistent metrics, and whenever there is doubt, people require proof. Simultaneously, the feminine (which is grounded by intuition rather than rooted in logic) is systematically devalued.

Remember when you played sports when you were younger and a boy would say, "You throw like a GIRL!" That was supposed to be an insult. He was trying to concretize the idea that anything having to do with girlhood, womanhood, or femininity is considered weak. Sadly, many of us heard these kinds of messages in everyday life, even in church. We did not celebrate the Divine Feminine because we were not taught about her intrinsic worth and value. Now that we are older and have agency, we can celebrate her. So, let's give her room to *breathe*.

Now, hear me: Feminine energy is not the same as femininity. We have somehow collapsed femininity into wearing pink, makeup, heels, and dresses. It is feminine energy, not femininity, that is the essence of the Divine Feminine. As Black women who, historically, have not been considered human, much less "woman," this is paramount for naming how our sacred bodies came to be considered sacrilege.

It has been a journey, but I have learned to reject any ideology that does not see my body as inherently good. I now

---

* I realize that this binary language is eurocentric and limiting. Everyone, regardless of how you self-identify or what gender pronouns you use (e.g., she/he/they), holds within a blend of both masculine and feminine energy to be complete. African and Black spirituality public scholar Juju Bae asserts that these concepts predate colonization and we must try our best to "see" them without the lens of gender and oppression.

know my body is holy (just as it is), and so is yours. After all, everybody is different. . . . Every *body* is different. Coming home to *your* body looks different for different folx: transgender, disabled, chronically ill. Your body *is* the temple of the Holy Spirit, and you deserve to feel whole in it.

I invite you to take inventory of what it is you believe you need to be whole. And that can look different at different turns. After all, healing is a process. This is not a one-time deal. Likewise, nurturing your intuition is not something that you master once and your work is done. Far from it! Dr. Estés reminds us:

> If the deep intuition says "Do this, do that, go this way, stop here, go forward," the woman must make corrections to her plan as needed. Intuition is not to be consulted once and then forgotten. Your intuition is not disposable——it is meant to be consulted at all steps along the way, whether the work be wrestling with an inner struggle, or completing a task in the outer world. It does not matter whether concerns and aspirations are personal or global, before all else, every action begins with strengthening the spirit.[8]

It is critical that we offer inquiry as our sacrifice at our intuition's altar, for she will not set us out on course with the destination fully known. This is extremely difficult for recovering control freaks who try to manipulate each variable of every situation.

We are so accustomed to having GPS access to all of our directions that we are unsure of what to do when the only navigation we have is "take the first step." When God calls us to do something without a litany of information, our knee-jerk reaction is to frantically ask:

Wait, where are we going?
Who all gon' be there?
What can I bring?
Whatchu wearin'?
Girl! What's the address? I'm just gonna put it in my
    GPS!

Imagine packing up your Honda Accord with your rose-gold luggage, red toy poodle, travel tripod, and your best friend for a road trip. You both ensure that the playlists are lit and the snacks are plentiful, but once you descend to the on-ramp to the highway, you look at each other and realize that neither of you knows where you are going! Sure, you might panic at first, but what would happen if you both decided to lean in to your intuition and then took calculated risks and inspired action?

Intuition is a superpower that nudges us which way to go, in real time. As we are navigating these deep waters of life, we receive spiritual downloads that prod us a bit to the left or a touch to the right or, the most difficult to attend to: stop, wait, pause. Perhaps an affirmation that will comfort you for the journey is this:

Your intuition doesn't just call you *from* something.
She calls you *to* something.

Imagine you're lying in bed talking to a new paramour. As you bask in the sunlight (both the star and your smiles) he asks you, "If you could only listen to three artists (including their entire discography) for the rest of your life, who would they be?" What a juicy question!

"Stevie Wonder!" you might exclaim—the immediate (and correct!) response. You might even follow it up with Lauryn Hill or the King of Kings, Beyoncé Giselle Knowles-

Carter. But then you sense an incoming image and Luther Vandross flashes across your mind.

"I don't know why, but I'm sensing Luther Vandross for some reason," you tell him. "And now Bob Marley is coming up for me."

"That's because Luther Vandross is number one!" he shouts emphatically.

In moments like this, you are, organically and subconsciously, leaning in to a psychic ability that allows you to sense another person's thoughts.

This doesn't just happen with men we're sexually attracted to, either. . . . It happens with Sistas, too.

I was at an intimate reception hosted by one of my mentors when I connected with another Black woman who was into holistic wellness and astrology. We exchanged phone numbers and made plans to meet up. During our first lunch date, she was telling me about some tumult she had gone through with her ex-husband. Midsentence, she realized she needed more napkins and went to grab them along with some plastic utensils. When she returned and sat down, we jumped right back into our chat:

"So, you were saying— Steve and . . . Chris?" I prompted.

She looked astounded. "No! Well, yes. I was talking about Steve, but Christopher is this guy that I just ended things with."

She hadn't mentioned Chris, but I had *heard* "Chris." And it wasn't loud—like your elementary school principal shouting morning announcements over the loudspeaker—it just popped up in my imagination, as if out of thin air. Moments like these are intriguing, yes, *and* they are indicative of a psychic gift (claircognizance) that I didn't even realize I had. It wasn't until I started to trust and honor my intuition that I began to recognize my *other* God-given gifts. Embracing my intuition didn't just heal my relationship with my body—it healed (and coalesced) my relationship with my spirit. That is because we cannot heal our bodies without healing our spirits. They are intertwined like a neat set of fresh Saturday-night cornrows.

If you grew up hearing Sunday sermons that demonized women and our divine gifts, let me be crystal clear, beloved. Your seeing, your hearing, your "knowing" is supernatural, ancestral, and *good*. The only demonic things are Western, eurocentric colonialism and American, anti-Black "Christianity" that amputated our sacred inheritance from us. Now is the time to rise up, go deep, and reclaim what is rightfully yours.

Your intuition is always wooing you, and you are worthy of the woo. Our self-worthiness will help us to overcome our social trauma. As we heal our relationship to ourselves, we overturn reckless behavior that does not nurture women and those who support us. When we tap into our spiritual practices from a place of inherent worthiness, we reject colonized Christianity's "whitemalegod," as coined by author Dr. Christena Cleveland in her book *God Is a Black Woman*.

Genesis 1:1 states, "In the beginning, God created the heavens and the earth." Then, in verse 2, it says that God created "while the Spirit of God hovered over the face of the deep." In the original language, the noun for "Spirit" in verse 2 has a feminine ending. Rev. Dr. Wil Gafney, American biblical scholar, Episcopal priest, and associate professor of Hebrew Bible at Brite Divinity School, reflects:

> When I discovered that God revealed Godself as male and female in the first two verses of the Scriptures and that, by tradition, God's masculine self-revelation is preserved in translation and God's

feminine self-revelation is obscured in neutral terms or subject to gender reassignment (thank you Saint Jerome), I became a feminist biblical translator.[9]

How can we expect to know the Divine without hearing the voices of women? How can we claim to experience the fullness of God when we exclude first-person narratives of girls? We have had to turn to extra-biblical resources in order to cobble together a fuller mosaic of what the Creator should look like: love, light, and liberation.

And if the Creator looks like love, light, and liberation, then we, too, mirror those same lovely attributes. If your current spiritual belief system includes *not* trusting yourself, I invite you to consider: How can you say that you trust God, but not trust the God in you? Your divine gift of intuition resides in you so that you may dwell in her. If you have heard your intuition before and didn't listen to her, don't be hard on yourself for it. Celebrate that you even heard her! In the words of my friend, womanist, survivor, and trauma-informed spiritual practitioner Donnecia Brown, "Forgive yourself for all of the ways that you dishonored your own divinity by thinking you could find God outside of yourself. Come home to yourself. God is waiting."

There is so much joy, freedom, flow, and ease waiting for you on the other side of coming home to yourself. This gift is not something that only I have. It is a gift that we *all* have. Our power lies within us. Let's do all we can to access that power.

Enhancing Your Intuition

We might not be able to control *every*thing but, y'all, there are many things that we *can* control. Start with practicing mindfulness in your body. You can't get clear on your intentions if your brain feels fuzzy.

> AND THE MORE IN TOUCH YOU ARE WITH YOUR BODY, THE MORE IN TOUCH YOU ARE WITH YOUR INTUITION.

Your gut influences your "gut." What you eat (or don't eat) has a bearing on your body, and how you feel in your body affects your spirit. Now, I am not shaming you into any particular diet. I don't care if you're vegetarian, pescatarian, or flexitarian. It doesn't matter to me if you are vegan, plant-based, or raw—I am simply encouraging you to eat intuitively and cleanly. Buy grass-fed, lean cuts of meat. Purchase organic produce when you can. Look for non-GMO labels so that you are not eating any food that has been genetically modified. Do your research on *every* food item— even if it's low-fat or gluten-free. I once saw "gluten-free" printed on a Flamin' Hot Cheetos bag! Just because a product is marketed as healthy doesn't mean it is.

Everything that you do is spiritual, even your workouts. Everything you do with your body is a reflection of what is going on in the spiritual realm. And the more in touch you are with your body, the more in touch you are with your intuition. Move your body in ways that feel good to you. And if you are disabled, differently abled, or deal with chronic pain or discomfort, align with what you *are* capable of doing. Whatever your level of ability, get to or stay at your version of fit.

In April 2014, I was working out (in a MOOD, hunny, and without warming up or stretching) and ended up tearing my right meniscus. I underwent surgery and two months of physical therapy. In that time, I went from using two crutches, to just one, to walking with only a knee brace. While my right knee felt about 90 to 95% back to normal, it couldn't take

pounding the pavement like it used to. I had to adapt my cardio workouts to my comfort and pain levels, and that allowed
me to show myself even more grace by moving in gentler
ways that felt *good*!

After walking and practicing yoga for a few weeks, I felt
stronger and ready for more intense workouts. So, I started
taking spin classes with Keith Thompson of KTX Fitness, and
that changed my life. I fell in love with the spirit of unity among
people (mostly Black folks) living their healthiest lives, getting
or staying fit to trap music. Spin pushed me mentally, physically, and spiritually! Our classes were like church: one rider
taking off with a double-time and, next thing you know, someone else "catches the Spirit" and we are hooting and hollering
and getting free. I loved the culture of spin so much that I became a certified spin instructor. You never know how getting
in tune with your body will open you up to new experiences
and even sources of income! If you've been meaning to try
salsa dancing, roller-skating, or hula-hooping, do it! It's an invitation to play, and play enhances your intuition.

We want to be confident and comfortable in our bodies,
and exercising at least three days a week will keep us healthy
and feeling saucy. A nice mix of yoga, stretching, and cardio
with an emphasis on strength training will provide your body
with the range of movement that will enrich your everyday life.
If you are huffing and puffing after you climb up one flight of
steps, Sis, perhaps you can start taking the stairs more often to
build up your cardiovascular endurance. Start viewing your
spiritual health as an extension of your physical health and
soon you will tap into movement that feels good to *your* body.*

---

* I also realize that exercise can help us stabilize our mental health. If
you are living with a syndrome or disorder that affects your ability (or
even desire) to work out, please consult a licensed mental healthcare provider. They can help you identify patterns and create new (and healthier)
responses for you.

Now is your time to tap into the holy *within* so you can proudly illuminate the holy *without*.

Reflect:

I praise you, for I am fearfully and wonderfully made. Wonderful are your works; that I know very well. (Psalm 139:14)

Celebrate:

Choose an afternoon and schedule two hours for yourself to go on an adventure. Don't plan anything; leave it entirely up to your intuition. You can walk, ride a bike, drive, or take public transportation (if it's safe for you to do so). Tune in with what you feel led to do and where you feel led to go. Ask God to give you clarity if you experience moments of doubt. After your "intuition field trip," grab your journal and jot down what came up for you. What was this experience like for you? What did you enjoy? What surprised you? What did you learn?

Affirm:

I am on the perfect path of alignment with my purpose.
I trust my intuition.
I strengthen my body with movement and
nourishing food.

Chapter 4

"But the Bible Says . . ."

*Acknowledging What Church
and Society Got Wrong*

I was at a conference during my final semester at Yale Divinity School when I met Art. While there were numerous plenaries and sessions to attend, I found myself near this handsome stranger more than once. After talking smack about who was the better spades player (me, of course) and hesitantly expressing romantic interest in each other, he asked me for my phone number, and we began a whirlwind romance.

Since I lived in New Haven and he was based in Atlanta, FaceTime was our preferred mode of communication. When we talked, I would typically place my laptop strategically on my bed so that he could see my face clearly. One day, though, he called while I was working at my desk. During the course of our conversation, I leaned back in my chair and crossed my legs in front of the screen. Art, catching a glimpse of my thighs, commented on how luscious they looked. I, instantaneously self-conscious about being a "stumbling block" to this "man of God," repositioned my body so that he could no longer see my legs. Church teachings had convinced me that I needed to shrink myself so that I would not "tempt" him with my body.

Despite the distance, Art and I got serious, and I relocated to Atlanta to attend Columbia Theological Seminary— and to be with him. By that point, we had been together for six months and had not been involved sexually. Neither of us were virgins, but we were practicing celibacy because I believed it was the "right" thing to do. As my love and desire grew for Art, my theological queries started. Was sex before marriage *really* bad if I was in a healthy, exclusive, committed relationship? I certainly didn't feel like it was bad whenever Art grabbed my hand to carefully guide me into his car, or when he kissed me tenderly on the lips before telling me he loved me.

During one of the many nights we spent in his dorm room, we made love for the first time. It was sweet and romantic. And immediately after we finished, instead of cuddling up with my beloved, I rolled over onto my side and cried. Art, warmly concerned, leaned over my shoulder and gently placed his forefinger to my cheekbones. He felt the warm trickle of tears and exhaled. "Oh, no." He felt horrible that I felt guilty for having sex. Here I was, a grown woman in a healthy, loving relationship, unable to take great pleasure and delight in expressing my sensual love for my man.

Sadly, I know I'm not the only one who has experienced the trauma of the church's teachings on sex and sexuality. So many of us have. You know the tears during the altar call, repenting for your "sin." The disconcerting thought that God does not love you anymore because you had sex. Torturing yourself with thoughts of *If only I could stop sinning like this!*

Body-Talk Is God Talk

"Black Christians are having sex. . . . They're just not talking about it," Rev. Dr. Leslie D. Callahan, phenomenal preacher, educator, and the first woman pastor of the historic St. Paul's Baptist Church in Philadelphia, made this declaration during one of our many enriching discussions. When I was a student pastor in seminary, Dr. Callahan was my supervisor and I appreciated her candid take on sex. I had just completed my second year and was learning how to integrate all the knowledge I had gathered in an effort to serve Black congregations. Our church members had started a Bible study on the book of Joshua—a book I had *just* finished a course on, so I was ready (big-ups to Rev. Dr. Carolyn J. Sharp,* who also counseled and prayed with me weekly; *and* she gave me a prophetic witness shout-out during the Class of 2012's commencement address).

While conducting research for one of my assignments, I'd come across an article by an older, white, male Jewish scholar that explored one of the most prolific characters in the narrative: Rahab. Rahab was your favorite sex worker's favorite sex worker who cunningly outwitted the Canaanite king and saved and protected Israel's spies. This is important to note because the Canaanites and Israelites were known enemies. The biblical passage tells how two Israelite spies were sent to Jericho to scout out the land. They needed to avoid the king of Jericho and stay "incog-negro," so they went to the town prostitute, Rahab, who hid them. She then

---

* Rev. Dr. Carolyn J. Sharp is a professor of Hebrew Bible. I had her father as a Spanish teacher when I was in high school! Wild.

lied straight to the city officials' faces when they came looking for the spies. Get that, the Israelites went to the woman
who had all the tea—and, in my theological mind, a fat ass!

This scholar posited that the Hebrew word *zonah,* typically translated as "prostitute," could also mean "innkeeper."
What?! The tea is piping hot, chile! What would it mean for
Rahab to have been a hotelier as opposed to a harlot? I was
carrying this information, discerning if I should broach this
topic at Bible study, and Dr. Callahan encouraged me to do
so. She firmly yet kindly assured me, "You have to trust your
congregation to go there with you." And so, modeling my
liberation-oriented pastoral care ministry after her own, in
the most gentle, kind, and compassionate way, I carefully led
our Bible scholars and theologians through an investigation
and integration of the text. To this day, that excavation remains one of the richest ministry experiences I've ever had!

Thank God for pastors who tell the whole truth with *love.*
We need more pastors, preachers, ministers, teachers, and lay
leaders like Dr. Callahan, especially when it comes to body-
talk. Because body-talk *is* God-talk.

I am frustrated by the lack of healthy, holistic conversations around sex and sexuality in and beyond Black religious
spaces. The Bible, the Black Church's central sacred text, is
BURSTING with opportunities to talk about sex! The problem is, we have been too afraid (or ill-equipped) to go where
the text is leading us. It's time to unearth the text and compel a
more compassionate retelling and understanding of Scripture.

Just turn to the book of Song of Solomon. The Quiet
Storm ain't got shit on the Song of Songs!

Here is the ultimate litmus test for your Bible. The King
James Version of the Bible translates Song of Songs 1:5 as "I
am black, but comely." The New King James Version keeps
it going with "I am dark, but lovely." Other versions go a little
something like this:

"Dark am I, yet lovely." (New International Version)
"I am dark but beautiful." (New Living Translation
    and The VOICE)
"I am deeply tanned, but lovely." (Amplified Bible)
"I am weathered but still elegant." (The Message)

All right . . . ENOUGH! This "Conjunction Junction, what's your function" is absurd. The lengths to which colonizers will go to ensure that anti-Blackness infuses an inherently liberative text is mind-boggling! Just think what constructive work one could do with that energy. You could, I don't know . . . eradicate world hunger, poverty, and transphobia?

Most biblical scholars use the New Revised Standard Version (NRSV) of the Bible. *This* accurate translation states:

"I am Black *and* beautiful."*

Do you see how differently that lands? In the NRSV, this African woman is beautiful *because* of her Blackness, not in *spite* of it!

The Song of Songs book was attributed to King Solomon because he was the prolific, dynamic writer of his time. But, actually, factually, at least 75% of the book's dialogue is voiced by an African woman. Unless Solomon had some C-cups, those lines in Song of Songs came from the mouth of a Sista. Yes, fam. Black women's intellectual property has been pillaged and canonized in the Bible like some ancient papyrus version of TikTok. Don't believe me? Just watch.

"Let him kiss me with the kisses of his mouth!"[1] Say WHAT? If King Solomon were the original writer and he is talking about his lover using the pronouns "him" and "his," perhaps King Solomon was on his Frank Ocean jawn and

---

* Emphasis my own.

living in the fullness of his same-gender-loving self* (which I'm not mad at); but, likely, this was a Sista writing about her bae. "Draw me after you; let us make haste,"[2] she continues. There were cocktails in his loincloth and shawty did not want to be tardy to the party!

Even though Christian tradition teaches it as such, this is *not* a book about how God loves God's people or how Christ loved the church.[3] The Song of Songs is "an ancient biblical love poem that speaks frankly of towering breasts, flowing black [locs], kissable lips, and the joy of sexual fulfillment."[4] This is a book about an erotic, passionate, healthy, consensual sexual relationship, and we should not be ashamed to explore its depiction of intimacy. This is a book that celebrates pleasure!

Translations and Body-Talk

How people interpret the Bible is just as important as who wrote it. There have been councils held on which books of the Bible to keep and which to toss. There have been magistrates with agendas who authorized self-serving translations of the Bible. This is why womanism is so critical. This sensual system of thought invites us to take on a hermeneutic of suspicion. A hermeneutic is how you interpret a text: your lens, if you will—our deeper shade of purple.[5]

I know many of us grew up in traditions that proclaimed, "You don't question God or the Bible," but I believe interrogating the text is a Christian's birthright. God is big enough for our questions and uncertainty. In fact, Isaiah 1:18 summons us, "Come now, let us argue it out." So when we come to the biblical text, it's preferred that you bring an investiga-

---

* "Same-gender-loving" is a term coined by activist Cleo Manago and is a culturally affirming description for Black gay and bisexual people.

tive lens. Because if we don't examine the Bible for ourselves, we can go our entire lives not really knowing the truth about this sacred text that is foundational for so many of our faith communities.

According to a Center for the Study of Religion and American Culture study, "The Bible in American Life," 55% of people surveyed said that they preferred the King James Version and 19% preferred the New International Version. In addition, about 40% of congregations reported that they use the KJV in worship.[6] Unsurprisingly, most people who read the Bible are Black women.[7] This data conveys how popular these versions are, and it suggests that most Black women in Black churches are reading these particular translations. Black women deserve to have life-giving translations and interpretations of the Bible available for their divine affirmation.

For this reason, if you are deeply committed to the liberation of Black women and femmes, you cannot leave out the Black Church. Black women are building entire moral and ethical frameworks around the King James Version of the Bible—a translation that was authorized by a bisexual man in 1611. Yes, Sis. King James was a card-carrying member of the LGBTQ+ community. And, guess what? That wasn't that long ago! Let's also reflect on what else was happening in 1611: the transatlantic slave trade, beloved.

White, eurocentric "explorers" came to African lands and colonized our people. They demonized, dehumanized, and brutally enslaved our ancestors. They came over on boats named *Jesus, Grace, Hope,* and *African Queen.* Slave owners mixed a deadly potion of the illusion of white supremacy and stark anti-Blackness and tried to stop our ancestors from engaging our indigenous spiritual practices. This whitewashing of the Bible and the Gospel led to the physical *and* spiritual colonization of our foremothers and forefathers.

As thinking spiritual beings, we must be mindful of not only who was *creating* these texts, but also who was *crafting* these texts. As seen in the Song of Songs verses above, every translation is inherently an interpretation. Whenever a scholar sits down to look at a text, they are bringing their own personal training, biases, prejudices, and agendas to the work. When we honor the fact that many Hebrew words have multiple meanings, it cracks open the Old Testament in rich and juicy ways. In some cases, there are up to nine possible translations of one Hebrew word, so the translator's selection gives a particular nuance to that sentence. It is a tricky dance to navigate. I'm shocked, but I'm not surprised. The Bible has been so co-opted that even though the NRSV is the best option, it's still not perfect. In seminary, I was trained to use the NRSV because, we were told, it is the most accurate translation of the text. However, Dr. Randall C. Bailey, the now retired Andrew W. Mellon Professor of Hebrew Bible at Interdenominational Theological Center in Atlanta, illuminates a major cover-up.

In *They Were All Together in One Place? Toward Minority Biblical Criticism,*[8] Dr. Bailey recounts a conversation that he had with Bruce Metzger, the general editor of the NRSV:

> I once asked Bruce Metzger, "When *regel* is clearly a reference to the male genitals in the Hebrew Bible, such as in Ruth 3, why did the NRSV still translate it as 'foot,' as opposed to 'penis'?" Metzger responded that the translation was not only for study but also for worship modes and that "you couldn't say 'penis' in the sanctuary."

When I was living in the Bay Area, I visited a church where the pastor refused to say "penis." He was a Black man leading a multicultural* congregation in an area of the country where only 2% of the population identifies as Christian. I get that it was a delicate space, but, sadly, this church was not an anomaly.

The pastor started out by reading a passage of Scripture about circumcision. Now, there's only one organ on the human body that is circumcised. When he started to expound upon the text, he got to the perfect place to mention genitalia. But, instead of saying "penis," he said, "and other parts of the body, which I would say, but children are present."

What's that face Black people make when we're confused? Yep . . . that's the one I made! I was completely dumbfounded. Here was a ripe opportunity for an influential community leader to name a body part that is clearly referenced in the Bible. How can we expect to normalize conversations about our bodies if we never hear the anatomically correct terms verbalized from the pulpit?

Equipped pastors are excellent conduits for awakening body-conscious languages within the congregations they shepherd. I grieve how differently that moment could have gone for the church members who were present that day. I wonder which survivors of a physical or sexual assault, which disabled people, which gender queer or trans folx would have been comforted by knowing that their church was brave enough to curate body-centered dialogue.

Embodied praxis matters because Jesus came enwrapped

---

* I struggle with "multicultural" churches because their congregations are usually predominantly white with a few families of color mixed in, and rarely are they an authentic blend of different cultural worship styles. In my experience, most churches that are not talking about race are *definitely* not talking about sex. Moreover, it is imperative that we have age-appropriate conversations about bodies so that we can keep our communities and our congregations safe.

in flesh. And beyond our humanity, our innate physicality lies within our liturgy, as well. Why do some churches still have physical Bibles in every row? Why are there elders who refuse to sing congregational hymn lyrics from the sanctuary screen? Why do some church members vehemently reject using a Bible app? Some people are deeply tied to paper and need to hear the rustle of pages turning. Our physical experience *matters*. And it's important to talk about it in healthy, holistic ways. Language matters, too!

By the way, I have said "penis" in the sanctuary. In fact, I have said "penis" in the pulpit—multiple times. And, at the time of this writing, I am alive to tell the story.

The Scam of Purity Culture

When it comes to the book of Ruth, the church taught us that the protagonist lies at the *feet* of Boaz, but when we look at the original Hebrew language, we find that *regel* ("foot, leg") "can be used as a euphemism for the sexual organs, male or female."[9] Scholars admit that "sexual overtones are present in the action of a woman uncovering a man's legs in the dark of the night and lying down."[10] On the one hand there "can be no doubt," but on the other hand, in their "opinion," it's "utterly improbable." Well, in MY opinion, that is a whole lot of mental maneuvering just to avoid having to face, identify, and name a woman's expressed sexuality in the Bible. *I* think Naomi knew what was up and she instructed Ruth to perform oral sex on Boaz. The fact is, we don't know what really happened that night on the threshing floor, but church teachings have removed any talk of sexual overtones, and misrepresented or even excluded this entire narrative.

I command us to elevate and amplify women's sexuality in the Bible so that Black church girls can elevate and amplify their own. Black Christian women have been flinging themselves on the altar of purity culture, tithing to churches that won't ordain them, and abstaining from sex all because of a toxic ideology cloaked in misogynoir and steeped in religious dogma.

Naomi Had a Point

When I was at my best friend's bachelorette party in Las Vegas, we were lounging in our luxury suite talking about men and sex (as Black Christian women are wont to do whenever we gather). We learned that every woman present who was either married or engaged was sexually active. All of the virgins and Sistas practicing celibacy were single. For the umpteenth time, I sat amidst Black women who desired to be in a loving partnership, but because they were taught to amputate their sexual selves from their spiritual selves, they were repelling the very relationships that they wanted! Now, I'm not saying that the way to get a man is through sex, but I *am* saying that sex is an important part of our romantic relationships. Remember our good Sis in Song of Songs? She "does not hesitate to announce her desires for her man, and she does not wait until marriage to fulfill them."[11]

But, to the women who were virgins or celibate, if you have sex before you're married, you're "damaged goods." (Isn't it odd that, somehow, men aren't considered damaged goods when *they* have sex before marriage?) Like scores of other women, I was inundated with purity culture teachings. Sunday after Sunday we heard that if you have premarital sex, you're going to hell. Our sexuality, a gift from God, was demonized by the church. We fell victim to the idea that the only way to express your sexuality is within the confines of a heterosexual marriage.

Purity culture programmed me to believe that my body

was "evil" and a "stumbling block" that caused men to sin. Never mind the fact that men have agency over their own eyeballs. I grew up in New York City, where it was normal to be ogled, catcalled, and "hollered at" on the daily. Street harassment in the form of "yo, shaw-tay!" or "hey, ma" was the norm for me, and it didn't matter WHAT I was wearing. It never does.

Facing this kind of aggression on a daily basis is traumatizing. Suffering this trauma in spiritual communities—which should be the embodiment of safe, sacred space—adds another layer of harm.

There's this false notion that one is "pure" and "innocent" if you abstain from sexual activity, but "evil" and "demonic" if you *do* engage in sexual activity. So you get trapped in this hypo-Christian marriage complex and get married just to have sex in a "bed undefiled," only to discover that first, you don't know what you're doing, and second, you're not that good at it.

That's because we don't talk about sex, so you don't know the mechanics of it. On top of that (no pun intended), you cannot hear "if you have sex before marriage you're going to hell," "you need to keep your legs closed," and "good girls don't give head" every Sunday for decades and think that, somehow, some way, you will transform into a sexual goddess by the time the ink dries on your marriage certificate. Sis, you will not experience a transfiguration on the mount of lust to shed all of those suppressive articles of faith. A lifetime of conditioning will not magically slide out of your psyche once you have a wedding band on your left ring finger.

The Disconnect

If we are going to reintegrate all of who we are, embracing our heritage is a great place to start. Decolonizing my Christianity and liberating my faith have been essential to negotiating church teachings with what feels good to me. Reclaiming your heritage and ancient spiritual practices could be just the thing to unlock your next level of self-love. And, according to professor and author Dr. Karen Baker-Fletcher, loving yourself "is the first order of business"[12] to loving God. You cannot shun the very people you descend from and love yourself. Therefore, loving your lineage is a crucial step to enacting your self-love journey.

Tragically, there's a disconnect between Black Christians and the Afrocentricity of the Bible. European colonizers were well aware of the power of African spirituality. In order to enslave our ancestors, slave owners attempted to amputate them from their culture. Their names, languages, and rituals were stripped away and replaced with a whitewashed version of the Christ figure and a not-so-holy translation of the Bible. Public scholar Juju Bae, who is also a medium, conjurer, and Hoodoo practitioner, posits: "As displaced African people, we have carried our praise and worship even as the deities may have changed. . . . We still be singing, we still be wailing, we still be running around, we still be speaking in tongues."[13]

There are clear ties between Black Church worship and ancient African spirituality. Running counterclockwise in praise is inherent in both practices. Shouting during service is reminiscent of the ring shout of our ancestors, and speaking in tongues is conjuring.* The founder of the ultraconservative Church of God in Christ (COGIC) denomination, Bishop Charles H. Mason, was a root worker and Hoodoo practitioner. The retention of African spiritual practices in

---

* Conjure, also known as Hoodoo or Rootwork, is a Black American religion. Some would describe it as "folk magic," but African belief systems are *religions*. They are not "folk," myths, or tales. We never talk about the Bible as "folktales."

the modern Black Church highlights diasporic ways of worship, particularly as seen in Black charismatic and Pentecostal churches.

Jesus was African. Which means he had an African mama and African aunties and was raised learning African ways of being, including his spirituality. In ancient West African traditions, ancestral veneration* is a key component of connecting to Spirit, yet many Black Christians mistakenly deem anything African-centered as wicked. I know, I used to be one of those "super-saved" people who, whenever I saw an African tribal mask, would declare, "That's demonic!" Yet, in his letter to the Hebrews, Paul talks about a great cloud of witnesses.[14] The Gospels lift up Moses and Elijah.[15] Why is it acceptable for us to venerate these biblical ancestors, but it's "demonic" for us to venerate our personal ancestors? The ones whose literal blood is coursing through our veins? Perhaps if we honored people who look like us instead of the whitewashed eurocentric versions, we could recognize the beautiful image of God in *all* of Creation. And who couldn't use a little more self-acceptance and self-love?

Speak Life

We come from an oral/aural tradition, and that means the spoken word holds worlds for us. Storytelling as seen in poetry, hip-hop, and "y'all remember when?" is an essential element of Black meaning-making. Preachers are modern-day griots whose responsibility it is to tell our stories in ways that uplift rather than indemnify us.

The fact that the sermon is arguably the most critical and influential moment in Black religious services illustrates the

---

* To "venerate" means to respect, honor, and lift up . . . *not* worship. This is a critical distinction.

need for the most liberative theologies to be known and made known. It is no wonder that the Body of Christ is stuck in a perpetual identity crisis when we consistently receive incendiary messages about who and what we are whenever we are in sacred spaces. We cannot refer to ourselves as "Christians" (which means "like Christ") and hate ourselves. Jesus was Black. Thus, you cannot be anti-Black and a Christian.

Which is why I am wildly confused by Christians who refer to themselves as the Body of Christ, but then demonize their own bodies. The Black Church, born in spite of colonization and out of a need for a free space to worship away from the white gaze, began to internalize the very oppression that our ancestors fought so hard to resist. We are only as free as the least liberated among us, and yet many Christians, regardless of race, hold on to antiquated belief systems that keep our people bound.

The Bible Is Not a Buffet

Homophobia, transphobia, and queerphobia have no place in our spiritual communities. And it's about time that we cease having gatherings by denominational leaders to determine whether or not our queer kin are loved by God. Conservative evangelicals will often point to the Levitical text in order to make their argument against homosexuality. But what they don't realize is that they are approaching the buffet of Scripture and cherry-picking their favorite menu items. We cannot look at the Bible à la carte. If we are going to have any integrity about this ancient, human-written text, then we need to honor that although the Bible was inspired by God, it was written by men, for men, at a particular time, with a particular agenda. Throughout history, colonizer-thinkers retranslated and repurposed the text, thus reshaping it over time. There are same-gender-loving relationships in the Bible, but many of these nuances have been tarnished by improper translations.

One of the passages people point to when they argue that homosexuality is a sin is Leviticus 17–26. Also known as the Holiness Code, it was written to give guidelines for the Hebrew Israelites' rituals and morals. However, it does not serve us to engage this text without locating it within its proper historic, cultural context. Scholars have noted that these chapters do not sound or read like the rest of the book, so they were obviously a later addition.[16] Even if we engage Leviticus as is, we must pay attention to *all* of the verses. Leviticus 11 says, "don't eat pork," but we're still frying up bacon, extra crispy, on vacation with the homies. The text says, "don't eat shellfish," but we're still going to Red Lobster, "for the seafood lover in you," for birthday dinners and graduation celebrations. The Bible says, "don't mix fabrics," but we witness a parade of pastel polyblend suits on Easter Sunday. How, Sway?? Make it make SENSE.

I never hear homophobic hell-adjacent "Christians" talking about *these* "abominations." And even for New Testament texts that are contorted to be anti-homosexuality, Jesus didn't really talk about sex and never condemns sexuality. So, are we going to be Christian or Paulean? The mental maneuvering to manipulate the text in such a way that God can love swine-slanging, shellfish-slurping, polyblend-rocking Christians but not same-gender-loving people of faith must stop.

Homophobia in the Black community is a particularly horrifying affront. We subject our beloved community members to traumatizing anecdotes and unnecessary vilification. Same-gender-loving humans have been in the Black Church since the beginning. Even if they were not out, they were about. Gay men are leading our praise teams and directing our choirs. Lesbian women are praise dancing and coordinating Easter plays. Black churches will take all of the LGBTQ+

folx's tithes and offerings, then turn around and forbid their partners from attending Sunday worship.

Leviticus is not a biblical text that condemns same-gender-loving people. That's what cisgender, heterosexual, patriarchal white men do. On the contrary, Leviticus actually admonishes us to care for the poor, the deaf, and the blind. But we are so culturally stuck on this "abomination" word that we don't see the call to liberation right there in the rest of the Bible! You want to talk about an "abomination"? I'll show you seven! Here, let Proverbs 6:16–19 read you for filth. Seven things are an abomination to the Lord:

> [16]There are six things that the Lord hates,
> seven that are an abomination to him:
> [17]haughty eyes, a lying tongue,
> and hands that shed innocent blood,
> [18]a heart that devises wicked plans,
> feet that hurry to run to evil,
> [19]a lying witness who testifies falsely,
> and one who sows discord in a family.

I know we are religiously acculturated to always have the "correct" answer, beloved, but "I don't know" *is* a valid response. God is big enough to handle our wondering and our wandering, even (especially!) around the Bible. And to be abundantly clear:

The Bible is NOT God.

"Taking the biblical text seriously does not mean elevating it to divine status; bibliolatry is as much a sin as any other form of idolatry," asserts Rev. Dr. Wil Gafney.[17] It can be big, open, scary terrain to think for yourself, but a thinking Christian is a faithful Christian. As my Sista-friend, author, essayist, and theologian Candice Benbow says, "God gave us the ability to think critically for ourselves." If your pastor does not allow you to critically analyze the Bible, you need a new pastor. In addition, you are worthy of a formally theologically trained, Spirit-led faith leader who is curious and deeply committed to the liberation of ALL Black people. Because once we start thinking critically, we are not met with resolutions, but, rather, more questions. And while that makes many of us uncomfortable, *that* is the beauty of faith. We do not respond to the Bible with single, solitary responses; instead, we explore the murky, unclear waters of a text that is sacred, yet flawed; holy, yet incomplete.[18]

I am so delighted I serve the God of the "I don't know" and "not yet." Because it's in my exploration that I meet the God of love and light and liberation. Wherever the Spirit of the Eternal One is, there is liberty.[19] So anyone or anything that hinders my liberation cannot be of God.

Re-membered

The word "religion" comes from the Latin word *ligare*. "Ligare" means "to fasten" or "to bind" and "re" means "to do something again." Religion should refasten or rebind us to God. Sadly, colonized religion has shaped Western society in the most unfortunate ways. Following the lead of Joshua Harris, who retracted the wildly sensationalized tenets he purported in *I Kissed Dating Goodbye*,[20] scores of blogs, articles, theses, and dissertations are being written about the traumatic nature of repressive anti-body teachings. Church and society have gotten a lot of body-talk wrong. And while I pray all wounded spirits are mended and recovering minds are in therapy, I am deeply concerned with how Black women's bodies have been at the bottom of this piling heap of disjointed human beings.

So many Black women urgently need to be re-membered, figuratively put back together, from this abuse. If we embrace our sensuality, we're labeled "jezebels." If we express our sexuality, we're called "hos." When, actually, being comfortable in your flesh is godly. If we truly want to heal beyond anti-Black-woman religious dogma, then we must reject every philosophy that does not affirm our beautiful Black bodies just as they are. We don't have to yield more time, space, or energy for self-degradation because of some religious leaders' internalized anti-Blackness and misogynoirist beliefs.

My hope for every Black girl, woman, and femme is that we leave our sacred spaces feeling a lot more like God and a lot less like gross.

Reflect:

He sustained him in a desert land, in a howling wilderness waste; he shielded him, cared for him, guarded him as the apple of his eye. (Deuteronomy 32:10)

Guard me as the apple of the eye; hide me in the shadow of your wings. (Psalm 17:8)

Celebrate:

Learning to love your body just as it is is a journey and *every* journey has stops and starts. The next time you are thinking a negative thought about your body, stop that thought and immediately start to say words of affirmation aloud. "Ugh! I'm so—" *Holy!* "If I could just lose—" *Worthy!* "My thighs didn't use to—" *Beauty!* When your interior dialogue begins to deteriorate, remind yourself that you are enough! This might take some practice so feel free to write words on Post-its and put them where you can see them. You can even create a personalized image in a design app (like Canva or Adobe Express). Use your current favorite photo of yourself and add words that you want to internalize about your body. Save it as the wallpaper on your cellphone, laptop, and desktop so that you see constant reminders of your most bodacious self throughout the day!

Affirm:

I am an expression of God on the earth.
Sensuality is my birthright.
I am holy, worthy, and beautiful.

Chapter 5

#MeToo, Sis

Healing Sexual Trauma and Fostering Resiliency

I have included a discussion of a childhood sexual abuse incident. If you have experienced childhood sexual abuse or believe reading about it would be unhealthy for you for any reason, please skip to the section titled "Black Girls Deserve Agency," starting on page 80.

My father stood in our kitchen wearing a white T-shirt and a towel wrapped around his waist with nothing underneath it.

"I know you're getting older and you might be curious, so . . . come." He held out his hand to me. My body felt like lead. Even at ten years old, I sensed that something was off. I glanced at his towel, then looked at the floor.

"No," I mustered.

"Ok, fine." And he left it—and me—alone.

This was the first time I had ever said no to my father's

sexual abuse. My dad had been molesting me for a few years. Mostly inappropriate "checks" to make sure I had cleaned myself properly. The abuse went on for about five years altogether and let me tell you: Being betrayed by the first person who was supposed to protect me not only polluted my romantic relationships with men, but also my spiritual connection to God.

Growing up in church as a victim of father-daughter incest was unnerving. On Sunday mornings I would hear references to "Father God" as protector, provider, and caretaker when my biological father was the complete opposite. I didn't have the language for it at the time, but I was experiencing cognitive dissonance. What I was being taught in Sunday school did not align with what I was experiencing every other day of the week.

In our culture, incest is a taboo topic. However, as many Christians refer to one another as "brothers" or "sisters" or "siblings in Christ," we must recognize the kinship theme of our tradition. We must acknowledge the harm caused by clergy and church and community members. After all, most sexual violence is perpetrated not by strangers but by the closest of biological, spiritual, or social kin.

According to the Rape, Abuse & Incest National Network (RAINN), "Every 68 seconds, an American is sexually assaulted and every 9 minutes, that victim is a child."[1] One in ten children will be sexually abused before they turn eighteen years old.[2] But when you start looking within communities of color, those numbers are even higher.

Black Women's Blueprint* has been conducting an ongoing study since 2011 and has found that at least 70% of Black girls are sexually abused before they turn eighteen years old.

---

* A sociological organization based in New York that has been researching Black girls and women and sexual trauma since 2011 (www.black womensblueprint.org).

Most Black church congregations are at least 70 to 90% women.[3] That means that at least half of Black church congregations' members were sexually abused before they were legally allowed to vote. There is a desperate need to address childhood sexual abuse, intimate partner violence, and domestic violence from (and beyond) the pulpit.

One of the ways I worked through this was the in-depth study I made the subject of my master's thesis. In "The Problem with 'Father' God: Incest as a Silent Killer in the Black Church," I examined how we can use poetry alongside Scripture to preach against childhood sexual abuse and male sexual violence. Since there are no first-person narratives of women or children in the canonized Bible, we can use a womanist lens to make poetry a sacred text. As a preacher and a poet, I am able to weave stories together so that we can reduce stigma and silence shame. After all, statistics don't always change people, but stories do. And, chile, do we have stories.

Sadly, as damaging as my father's abuse was, he was not my sole perpetrator. When I was in elementary school, a boy a few years older than me groped my vagina and buttocks several times. I remember both liking and hating his touch at the same time. At school, some students would grab other students' breasts while covering their own and shout, "Titty attack!"

And it wasn't just child-on-child harm, either. Pedophilia in the West Indian community is another gross illustration of the adultification and hyper-sexualization of girls of the African Diaspora. My aunt's thirty-six-year-old Caribbean boyfriend made sexual comments toward me when I was fifteen. He even touched the small of my back once, but I left the room we were in (my aunt's bedroom . . . YIKES) and never let myself be alone with him again after that.

I know I am not the only survivor of male sexual violence who has experienced multiple assaults. Take a deep, cleansing breath, Sis. I see you.

In 2006, Tarana Burke launched the "Me Too" movement to let survivors of male sexual violence know they were not alone. She was particularly interested in serving Black girls in the Bronx, like herself and her daughter, who needed culturally relevant resources in order to heal and evolve.

So on October 15, 2017, when actress Alyssa Milano took to Twitter and asked followers who'd been sexually harassed or assaulted to reply with "me too," it set off a firestorm of storytelling. What followed was a moment of reckoning that added new fuel to the fire that Burke had blazed a decade before. Labeled with the hashtag #MeToo, millions of stories of rape, molestation, sexual harassment, street harassment, and gender-based violence were posted in response to Milano's tweet. I am certain that for every story that was shared, there were dozens of others that were not, and understandably so.

Whenever I share my stories of abuse, people always tell me, "You're so brave." Why is it brave for me to simply tell the truth? Because our culture has a poor practice of blaming victims and protecting perpetrators. The blaming and shaming that most survivors suffer is often a retraumatization on top of the actual incident. When victims come forward, people often ask incriminating questions like:

What were you wearing?
How much did you drink?
Why did you go back to his place?

Our cultural norm is to put the survivor on trial, as opposed to the perpetrator. Beloved one, if you have been sexually violated, I want you to hear me: Sis, I see you. I hear you. I acknowledge you. And I believe you. What happened to you was wrong, it wasn't your fault, and there was nothing you could do to stop it or prevent it. God is pissed about it. Your ancestors are pissed about it. And I'M pissed about it!

The silence, stigma, and shame that most pastors and spiritual leaders put on the victims of violence is sinful. As my therapist, Dr. Briana Boyd, helped me to see, when survivors come forward, we are asking for belief, accountability, and justice. We are asking bystanders to *do* something. Meanwhile, the perpetrator tries to minimize, deny, or ignore what happened—essentially asking bystanders to do nothing. So what's easier for bystanders: to admit that their favorite pastor, preacher, minister, deacon, uncle, line brother, or coach is a sexual predator, or to keep living in their fantastical world where they convince themselves that "he couldn't do something like that"?

For decades the church's response to sexual assault has been abysmal. Today, as the church reckons with more and more disclosures of sexual abuse at the hands of community members, it has a moral obligation to create safe space for victims and survivors of childhood sexual abuse. Additionally, the church must work to raise awareness of and end male sexual violence. While the church's tradition has often been one of collusion and cover-ups (the Catholic Church, Hillsong[4]), our post-#MeToo culture requires people of faith to do all they can to protect the most vulnerable among us.

Facing the Horror

A part of the horror of male sexual violence is the minimizing we do in our own lives. I have met victims of male sexual violence who did not know they were actually victims. Language matters, as does meaning-making. Sexual violence means different things in different states, but for the sake of this book, I use RAINN's definition. According to their website, "Sexual assault is any sexual contact or behavior that occurs without explicit consent of the victim." Consent means that you are giving your hearty "ok" or approval to partake in an activity. If no consent was given for the sexual contact or behavior, then it is sexual assault.

Maybe it's a pastor who invites an overwhelmed female congregant to his study and, instead of counseling her, he rapes her. Perhaps it's the youth minister who molests the very children he was charged to teach and protect. Or maybe it's the deacon who, during the congregational greeting on Sunday morning, grazes your breast as you lean in for a holy hug.

While I know that there is a critical mass of pastors, preachers, teachers, lay leaders, and congregants who are ready, willing, and able to labor to heal sexual trauma and end sexual assault against girls and women, our communities are simply not doing enough to systematically address Black women's mental, spiritual, psychological, social, and theological woundedness.

The church can no longer afford to offer survivors reckless religious platitudes like:

It happens to everyone.
Just let go and let God.
You need to forgive and forget.

Forgiveness is inherently confrontational. One who has been cut cannot forgive anyone or anything if the offender and the surrounding community members do not even acknowledge the laceration. What happens is that, over time, we become so accustomed to the abuse of Black girls and women that we begin to normalize it. "Rather than confronting rape, exploitation, and re/presentation, during and after slavery, rupture, incest, and assault,"[5] the church has normalized and even theologized the abuse of women and girls. Child molestation should not be the norm. Putting the survivor on trial can never be the protocol. Blaming a survivor, especially one who is honest enough to disclose her sexual assault, is reprehensible. Questions like these should never be part of the dialogue with a survivor:

> Do you want to ruin his life?
> Did you do anything to provoke him?
> Were you walking?
> Talking?
> Blinking?
> Breathing?
> Existing?

When victims are forced to search for their role in their own assault and survivors are warped into scapegoats for their rape, it's no *wonder* 80% of sexual assaults go unreported.[6]

Sexual assault is also highly unreported because many Black girls and women do not even acknowledge their sexual assault. We tend to downplay our experiences if we're not supported when honoring our truth. That's because some types of sexual assault are more covert than others.

> ONE WHO HAS BEEN CUT CANNOT FORGIVE ANYONE OR ANYTHING IF THE OFFENDER AND THE SURROUNDING COMMUNITY MEMBERS DO NOT EVEN ACKNOWLEDGE THE LACERATION.

Coercion

So you and boo thang are kissing and tonguing and feeling and groping. He reaches for the button of your high-waisted skinny jeans and you swat his hand away. "No." You are clear. He comes back with, "Oh, but, baby, don't you like it? Don't you love me? You know you want to." This wearing-down-until-you-finally-relent is a form of sexual assault. This is why enthusiastic consent is so critical. (More on that later in this chapter.)

Stealthing

There are many people who prefer sex without a condom. However, in order to prevent the transmission of STDs, STIs, and unwanted pregnancies, they strap up because it's the healthy, responsible thing to do. Yet there are men who are so dangerously inconsiderate that they will put on a condom before penetrating their partner and, just before they enter, take off the condom. It's called "stealthing" and it's a form of sexual assault. If you notice this happening to you, it is your right to demand he stop immediately. Your body, your rules.

Sadly, many Christian women do not know they have the right to implement boundaries around their bodies, much less how to enforce them. Many of us simply did not grow up having a sense of agency for ourselves. We were raised, instead, with these perilous imperative refrains:

Sit down.
Cross your legs.
Be a lady.

Black Girls Deserve Agency

The directives we received as young girls have shaded our social interactions as grown women. We were conditioned to listen to everyone else's input about our bodies and how we were "allowed" to show up in the world. We were taught at a young age that we were supposed to do as our elders said, even if it made us feel uncomfortable. Think about the times when you were forced to hug family members you simply did not like. "Don't be rude! Give your uncle a hug," your aunt would press. Our own family convinced us we did not have agency over our bodies. Our communities must transform so that we raise our girls with a sense of self-possession, not self-denial.

Girls taught to trust their intuition will divinely align with their own sense of agency. Whether we listen to her or not, our intuition usually lets us know what's up. I know I already covered how important nurturing our intuition is, but I'm affirming it here. You know the family friend, coach, or youth pastor that you didn't like, but you weren't sure exactly why? That deep "knowing" was your gut, the Holy Spirit, your inner compass guiding you. And yet we have been religiously trained to not be in tune with her. The abuse of women is perpetuated by the abuse of the Divine Feminine. I can't say it enough, there is no life without women's bodies. We can only have gender-based violence in a world that does not value gendered bodies. This is why God-talk is so pervasively patriarchal: "Father God, in the name of Jesus." Where is the woman in that?

Remember, the Holy Spirit is a divine feminine being, so you cannot believe in the Holy Trinity and be sexist. In Chapter 3, I pointed out that the Spirit that hovered over the face of the deep in Genesis was a woman. Similarly, Sophia (which means "wisdom" in the Bible) has a feminine ending. Dr. Will Coleman, author of *Tribal Talk: Black Theology, Hermeneutics, and African/American Ways of "Telling the Story,"* posits that wisdom is a divine entity unto herself—an expression of the African Divine Feminine that calls us into relationship with the womanly attributes of God.

"Women *have* wisdom. Men *acquire* wisdom," Coleman

> RAPE CULTURE CONVINCES US TO TEACH GIRLS "DON'T GET RAPED" INSTEAD OF TEACHING BOYS "DON'T RAPE."

ruminates. This language matters, especially when it comes to gender-based violence. In order to heal, we must face, identify, and name the truth. We can't just say "sexual violence." That is too nebulous a phrase; it does not place responsibility where it belongs: squarely on the shoulders of perpetrators and those who support rape culture.

"Sexual violence" makes it seem like there is some headless monster roaming around dark alleys, when the majority of sexual predators are, indeed, men. Yes, women are perpetrators, too, but by and large, most rapists are men.[7] This is significant language, because it urges us to specify, as author and activist Jason Katz suggests, "male sexual violence." That distinction helps us behead the demon.

This course-corrective language can have a significant impact on destroying rape culture. Rape culture, per Rev. Dr. Neichelle Guidry, is not about one single act of male sexual violence; rather, it is about discourse, a system of beliefs, the words we use, and a line of thinking that often begins with questioning the victim.[8] Rape culture protects the perpetrator and blames the victim. Rape culture convinces us to teach girls "don't get raped" instead of teaching boys "don't rape."

Right now, our culture is raising rapists—even in the church. While a culture remains the same, with help, I am hopeful that, by following the steps below and being a community committed to wholeness and liberation, we can change the status quo to one in which we cocreate a more just, equitable, *healed* world. Imagine a world where our exchanges no longer sound like:

"Hey, how's it going?"
"Good. You?"
"Fine."

And, instead, sound something like:

"Hey, how's it going?"
"Not good. I'm triggered."
"I am sad you're having a tough time. . . . How can
I support you?"

I dream of a world where we cocreate sacred, brave, rela-
tional space for one another where we can be honest about
not being well and have completely transparent exchanges
with one another. I dream of a time when a Sista, triggered
by realizing her coworker's cologne is the same as her assail-
ant's, will be granted the afternoon off to go care for herself.
I envision a moment when a collegiate, after seeing her rapist's line brother in the cafeteria, can receive tender support
from campus administration. I am conjuring a world where
a trans sister finds a movie ticket stub from *that* night and
won't be obliquely questioned, "You haven't forgiven him
yet?"

Black women deserve better. "Black women and girls
support the Black Church and its institutional and cultural
productions because they believe it will aid them in making
sense of their lives. . . . Yet the Black Church is guilty of violence against Black women and girls."[9] We are owed complete
and holistic care by the institution we've built. It is our money
that gives breath and our labor that gives life to the Black
Church. Black women deserve to be nurtured, not used.
There are still many Black churches that don't ordain women,
but gladly accept tithes from women and enlist them to clean

all the toilets, design all the programs, and usher all the people. They will accept Black women's leadership, but will *still* call them "Sister" instead of "Minister," "Beautiful" instead of "Reverend," or "Evangelist" instead of "Pastor." It's enough to make you want to march your stiletto-clad feet right out the church doors.

If the Black Church is ever going to be a place of sacred healing for all, we **must** be honest about the texts of terror[10] in our faith communities, both written and lived. Pastors, preachers, and teachers who justify rape by calling women and girls "stumbling blocks" need to be held accountable for their vile and dangerous dogma, especially when their formulaic thoughts are indicative of their insufficient engagement with sacred texts.

Male Sexual Violence in the Bible

We cannot deny that there are incidents of male sexual violence in the Bible. Idolizing King David completely sidesteps that he was a treacherous, murdering rapist. In 2 Samuel 11:4, the Hebrew text says that David "seized" Bathsheba.[11] Does "seize" sound consensual to you? This was not some hot, steamy, adulterous love affair. If Bathsheba had denied the king's command, she would have been killed on the spot. So, no, darling ones—Bathsheba could *not* have just said no. Moreover, God punished David for his heinous act; God did not punish Bathsheba. That tells us that Bathsheba did nothing wrong.

If we have biblical translators who replace "penis" with "feet" (as in the

> MOREOVER, GOD PUNISHED DAVID FOR HIS HEINOUS ACT; GOD DID NOT PUNISH BATHSHEBA. THAT TELLS US THAT BATHSHEBA DID NOTHING WRONG.

book of Ruth), then how can we expect the church to be honest about rape? It angers me to know that pastors, preachers, and priests who learn these truths in seminary continue to perpetuate dangerous lies about our bodies from the pulpit. They are committing spiritual malpractice and do not deserve to be in ministry. Christian women who have suffered male sexual violence are worthy of holistic healing and support.

Sis, *you* are worthy of care.

Beloved, God cares. Your ancestors care. I care. Darling one, you deserve to be seen, heard, and believed. You are welcome to question and be angry *with* God. You can cry, scream, kick, cuss, and fuss with God—whatever will help you to honor and process your pain. Believe me when I tell you that God did not let your sexual assault happen to make you "stronger." You did not need this "trial" to make you a better Christian. The deification of suffering is especially dangerous when it is force-fed to survivors.

> THE DEIFICATION OF SUFFERING IS ESPECIALLY DANGEROUS WHEN IT IS FORCE-FED TO SURVIVORS.

We Are "Surthrivors"

One of the most liberating experiences I had in seminary was learning about theodicy. Theodicy is the existence of evil alongside a good God. In his senior sermon at Yale Divinity School, my dear friend and professor of homiletics, Rev. Dr. Kyle Eugene Brooks, contemplated, "Why do bad things happen to good people? Because bad things happen to all people." Sometimes downright gory things happen to us and we fear facing them. But, if we are willing to go where the word of God takes us, then we can certainly go from victims to survivors to *Surthrivors*.

When I was in seminary, and I started engaging sexual assault statistics and stories, I kept seeing this word "survivor." Though I identified as one, "survivor" felt so flat to me. I was in divinity school full-time studying theology and religion, in deep community with brilliant, loving beings, and was an acclaimed spoken word and slam poet. I wasn't just surviving, I was *thriving*!

So I took it upon myself to coin a more accurate term: **Surthrivor**, one who flourishes despite facing life's harsh, extenuating circumstances. We need the Destiny's Child reunion so they can make the "Surthrivor" remix!

People ask me all the time how I got into this work. It's because I wanted to heal my sexual trauma. I found that the church did not know how to hold space for me so I could rage and grieve all that was lost and taken from me. I was nineteen years old when I made my first attempt at counseling. It was with a Catholic priest who did not offer me room to share authentically. When I was in my early twenties, I remember telling my assistant pastor's wife that my dad had sexually abused me. "Oh, that's a demon," she proclaimed. I remember thinking, *No . . . it wasn't a demon. It was my dad. He has a body and an address and a social security number.*

I learned that whether I was in a Pentecostal church known for magnificent praise breaks or a Baptist church with a phenomenal social justice ministry, clergy and church members alike were ill-equipped to handle my needs. Whenever it came time for prayer requests, we could ask God for healing from sickness, safety for surgeries, securing of new jobs, passage of safe travels, and comfort for the bereaved. But I never heard anyone praying for victims of childhood sexual abuse or survivors of male sexual violence. Modern church culture employs language that speaks of God's power to "heal," "save," and "restore," but rarely actually names the evils of rape, molestation, and assault. Granted, we do not want to list off a litany of abuses and cause more harm to our congregation members; but at what point are we willing to trust God to walk with us through the valley of the shadow of death?[12]

When it comes to confronting sexual abuse, God is willing, but the church is weak.

We can strengthen ourselves for the journey by transforming the language of our liturgy and creating safe, protected spaces in our churches. The worship center in a church building is called the "sanctuary." A sanctuary is "a safe or holy place." It is not our fog machines or LED lights that make our churches holy. If they are not safe, they are not sanctuaries. We must take thoughtful steps to change church culture so that we can raise awareness, create spaces of healing for survivors, and put an end to childhood sexual abuse and male sexual violence for good.

Consent Is Your Birthright

Teaching consent is a simple way to invite conversations about our bodies, our agency, and how we navigate these delicate conversations in community. But, consent is not something that the Black Church has historically done well. It's not uncommon to hear phrases from the pulpit that sound something like:

"Touch us, Father."
"Use me, Lord."
"Break us, oh God."

We sing hymns with these words not realizing the violence we are embodying. A popular young Black woman gospel artist's lyrics include "I feel a beating in the Spirit." This is absolutely terrifying liturgical language that the Black Church must overhaul. These invasive expressions condition us to believe that our bodies are meant to be harmed by God, and that is dangerous conditioning.

Y'all, consent is biblical. In Luke 1:38, Mary, not a thirty-year-old white woman but a thirteen-year-old Black girl, says, "Let it be with me according to your word." Mary consented to being impregnated by the Holy Spirit. She, a teenager, models how even children have, and should be empowered to enact, their own agency. God honored that Mary, a Black girl, had a choice over her own body; and Mary, in turn, after thoughtful consideration, consented to God's call. Consent, beloved one, is your birthright.

We must examine the missteps of our childhood faith if we are ever going to course-correct. During the welcome portion of worship services, very few people are asking for permission before they reach in for a full-frontal embrace. Preachers histrionically proclaim, "Touch your neighbor!" but do not admonish that you should receive consent before high-fiving, hugging, or grabbing someone. And for those of you who are thinking, *It's not that deep,* I invite you to listen to the Sistas in your congregation who have been sexually assaulted *inside* their church!

> CONSENT,
> BELOVED ONE,
> IS YOUR
> BIRTHRIGHT.

Here is a quick teachable moment: Next time you want to hug someone, try asking rather than assuming that your hug is welcomed. If we can talk about why consenting to hugs matters, we will inevitably get to consenting to sex. It is a small but effective way to unpack the baggage we inherited about our bodies and begin to heal, so that the church can be a survivor-centric, *truly* safe, sacred space. A place for Surthrivors.

The more we learn the language of consent, the more

fluently we will speak it in our everyday lives, *especially* in our romantic relationships.

The first man to ever ask me for consent was a man I went to high school with and later dated, Greg. We were kissing in a park. I was sitting on a concrete wall and he stood between my legs. As his fingers crept under my denim miniskirt, up my thigh, and closer to my clitoris, he whispered in my ear, "Should I be stopping?" It was a common refrain whenever we were physically intimate, and I loved it every time.

Another former beau, Demond, a gem I met on OkCupid, was hovering on top of me in his bed. We were kissing (do you see a theme here?) and grooving when he began to kiss on my chest, breasts, and stomach. He paused, gazed up at me longingly, and silkily asked, "Is it ok for me to keep going?" Y'all, I promise you, I almost came right then and there! "YES!" I exclaimed. I was even more turned on because consent is sexy, fun, and HOT! It is my prayer that every sexually active adult engages consent as a spiritual practice.

#BlackChurchToo

In the wake of the #MeToo movement, progressive evangelical Christian leaders implemented the #SilenceisnotSpiritual campaign. It was a way to bring the reckoning that took place on Twitter to the church. As I am socially located in the Black Church, I amplify the #BlackChurchToo movement.

The #BlackChurchToo movement is of critical importance because Black Christian women survivors must heal and mend their images of their sexuality and bodies. Trauma can impact our self-esteem, which, in turn, distorts our self-image. Black women need to hear core messages of inherent beauty, worthiness, and divinity from the pulpit. That's why it is so important to center womanism in both preaching and praxis—so survivors can hear how deeply God loves them and then grow to love themselves, unapologetically, in and beyond their spiritual communities.

Our Voices Are Holy, Too

Black churches that pride themselves on being "Bible-based" wrongly use the epistle letters from Paul to justify not having women in church leadership. When Paul wrote to the church at Corinth that "women should be silent in the churches,"[13] he was referring to the timing of their questions, not that they need to hush up in church. The passage is about orderly worship and curating a cohesive church service. Women, who were new to the worship experience, had questions about what was happening in the service. They would ask their husbands about the various elements in the middle of worship to make sure they knew what was happening. It's kind of like when you're on time to church and get your favorite spot in the pew only to have to make way for latecomers during the first appropriate pause in liturgy.

It was a small, minute inconvenience that concerned Paul because he wanted the entire community to have a nourishing spiritual gathering. It had nothing to do with a patriarchal agenda to mute women and exclude them from church leadership. If you are craving culturally relevant, spiritual leadership, I would invite you to visit churches that have women on the ministerial staff. We will not be the complete "Body of Christ" if many members are missing.

To be a Christian means to be "Christlike" or "like Christ." Jesus never demonized sexuality. Jesus never said, "silence the children" or "oppress the women." In fact, his words, his life, and his work elevated the exact opposite!

When it comes to radical inclusion, wholeness, and healing, we could stand to be more like Christ.

This does not mean to minimize your experience and betray yourself, however. Being a Christian does not mean you have to jump to forgiveness right away. You get to be angry about your sexual trauma. You get to be mad at God. And you get to heal yourself at your own pace. One day, telling the truth won't be considered brave. Even—especially—when that truth is pretty ugly. Here's to being a wide-open portal of truth and a gateway to healing.

Reflect:

To give unto them beauty for ashes, the oil of joy for mourning, the garment of praise for the spirit of heaviness. (Isaiah 61:3, KJV)

Celebrate:

Sister survivors, we heal by the love of God, the support of our ancestors, and the care of our community. We unravel in therapy and we crumble in prayer. We also overcome by "the word of [our] testimony."[14] I'm not saying that you need to broadcast every single detail about your assault(s) on social media, or that you need to disclose your perpetrator (you're welcome to do so, if you'd like, but you don't have to). If you're comfortable enough, share your story with one person you trust. If you're not there yet, perhaps you'd like to journal about it (you can even tear the page out and shred it or burn it so that you don't see it every time you open your notebook). Anything that helps you to face, identify, and name the truth will put you squarely on the path to wellness. You cannot heal what you do not reveal.

If you have not experienced male sexual assault (praise God!), I invite you to take steps to make sure that your church is a safe space for women and children. Ask your pastor to preach against male sexual violence. Check in with the children's ministry leadership to confirm that volunteers are given background checks. Make sure volunteers are trained to identify, prevent, and address childhood sexual abuse. I've had family members and even former schoolteachers ask me why I never told them about my abuse. My question to them is: Why weren't you a person I could tell? Be a person we can tell.

Affirm:

I am worthy of consent.
I am safe.
I can heal from sexual trauma.

Chapter 6

Feel the Feels

Honoring Your Body's Truth

When I got pregnant in November 2019, I was thrilled! Sure, my child's father and I weren't together, but he was tall, fine, rich, funny, and smart. The PERFECT baby daddy! But my joy was short-lived when, upon learning that I was pregnant, he ghosted me. Soon after this seemingly perfect match for coparenting showed me that he was a complete coward, the unfathomable happened.

It was a typical tranquil Sunday morning. I woke up without an alarm clock and went to the bathroom. As I sat down on the toilet seat, to my horror, I discovered bright red blood in my underwear. I called my doula and she reassured me that spotting in early pregnancy is normal. My dear friend and confidante Marcell echoed my doula's sentiments and shared that his former spouse had experienced early spotting during her pregnancy. He also nudged me to visit the emergency room and get checked out, just to be safe.

After a pelvic exam, sandwiched between two sono-grams, the doctor told me that while my embryo had shifted between my two assessments, my cervix was still closed. She called it a "threatened abortion." Apparently, my sac never implanted in my uterine wall, so I had to play wait-and-see. I was ordered to take forty-eight hours of bed rest, then return to the ER for a follow-up visit.

The next day, I called my OB/GYN and spoke to a mid-wife, who instructed me to drink tea and eat soup and "lots of nourishing foods." I don't know if it's because it was two days before Christmas, but it seemed like no one wanted to tell me what was really going on with my body. On December 23, 2019, I experienced intense abdominal cramping and lower back pain. At that moment, I knew—I went from being a vessel to being hollow.

The next day, Christmas Eve, I sat in the waiting room, looked down at my deflated breasts, and I could just tell. I was no longer pregnant. I had been just five weeks along.

While it might be considered quite early, I'd already told my closest loved ones (about thirteen people altogether) that I was pregnant. The week before I miscarried, I was getting ready to share the news with more friends because I was excited that our village was expanding. I even stumbled across a sale at Anthropologie (one of my favorite stores) and bought two dresses to accommodate my anticipated basketball belly the following summer. One was a flowy ce-rulean silk wrap dress that was two sizes too big, and the other a black knee-length bodycon with a sexy side slit, which would give me room to stretch, grow, move, and *breathe*. Listen here, your girl was NOT about to be buying NOBODY'S maternity clothes! I was very much giving Rihanna maternity vibes before my Bajan cousin even got pregnant.

When I'd popped in to T.J. Maxx to buy some candles (my Marshalls, HomeGoods, Ross, Big Lots, and World Market ministries are STRONG), I found myself wandering around the baby clothes section. I felt in my spirit that I was having a boy, but I bought gray onesies anyway, because I wanted to embody the wonder of not knowing my growing baby's sex. Plus, onesies are just so stinking cute!

Some people would have admonished me not to buy onesies just yet: "Don't get *too* excited; wait until the first trimester is over." But even waiting for the thirteenth week of pregnancy does not guarantee you're going to carry your baby to term.

> DON'T ALLOW THE POSSIBILITY OF LOSS TO STOP YOU FROM ENJOYING THE EXCITEMENT OF WHAT *IS*.

Whenever we receive exciting news, we should be able to share it. *Especially* if it's something as exhilarating as pending motherhood. I urge you, don't allow the possibility of loss to stop you from enjoying the excitement of what *is*. Whenever something—or someone—exists, it doesn't matter how long they were here. All that matters is that they *were*. As my ancestral teacher, Sobonfu Somé, declares, "Grieving is not synonymous with being weak. It is a source of strength, love, and power. It is a sign that the relationship had something valuable and irreplaceable in it."[1]

Don't allow social conditioning to minimize your excitement. People who love you will want to celebrate with you, and, if the unthinkable happens and you miscarry, those same people will want to hold space for you. Who does it serve to keep your pregnancy quiet until it's "safe"? How many mothers (and fathers and parents) are grieving this incredible loss alone, angry, and ashamed? If you want to announce your pregnancy at twelve weeks, announce at twelve. If you want to announce your pregnancy at five weeks, announce at five. If you want to announce right when you pee on that stick and see a plus sign, do YOU!

Sadly, at least 25% of all pregnancies end in miscarriage,[2] but I didn't know the number was that high until I had my own. When I posted my story on social media, I was buoyed with love and support from my community, *and* I was also overwhelmed with comments, direct messages, and text messages from women and men who had experienced pregnancy loss.

I had NO idea so many people had been grieving, silently and alone. It's difficult to know how to express the fact that you're grieving someone you've never met—especially when most people didn't even know they existed. How do you grieve in a culture that does not embrace mourning? How do you grieve in a society that does not know how to sit with pain, anguish, and lament?

Our cultural compass points toward removing discomfort as quickly as possible. Miscarriage makes people uncomfortable, especially in the church. But pregnancy loss is already exhausting enough. Angel moms* who lose their children in utero should not have to worry about protecting other people's feelings about their miscarriage. And while folks mean well, reciting platitudes exacerbates rather than alleviates the pain. I was horrified whenever someone told me things like:

"God needed another flower for his garden."
"At least you know you can GET pregnant."
"You can always try again."

---

* A woman who has lost a pregnancy is affectionately called an "angel mom."

Well-meaning Christians continuously added insult to injury. Their painfully placating overcompensation made me want to fight someone.

No, "he" didn't.
<u>That doesn't matter.</u>
I don't want to try again. . . . I want the one I had.

I wasn't just grieving a pregnancy—I was grieving the life I lost (the baby) and the life I lost (as a mom).

Healing Pregnancy Wounds

It is imperative that we have conversations about pregnancy and infant loss in and beyond the Black Church, so we can support grieving parents. We need our community to be able to hold us while we wail celebrating on would-be birthdays. And we need our loved ones to honor us on Mother's or Father's Day. I know miscarriage can be unpleasant to talk about, but angel mothers' lifelong comfort is more important than your temporary discomfort.

Being a Black angel mom is especially difficult because, while the Black community reveres motherhood, we don't know yet how to embrace bereaved angel mothers. Black angel moms deserve to be seen, heard, affirmed, and cared for. In my grief, I tried to make sense of how out of control I felt. *I took too many ginger shots* or *I shouldn't have worked out so hard at the gym.* The cruelest thought I had was, *Maybe God is punishing me for having multiple abortions.*

While not every woman who chooses to terminate her pregnancy feels remorse, I experienced layers of shame that were attached to my prior-terminated pregnancies. At eighteen, nineteen, and thirty-one, I found myself pregnant and unprepared to be a mother. Due to the shame that many misguided people heap upon women who receive this medical procedure, I ultimately found myself diving headfirst into a huge pile of guilt. My pastor, Rev. Dr. Maisha Kariamu Handy,* helped me to remember that God is not vengeful; and God would not take something as precious as my baby away from me because I had chosen not to enter motherhood before I was confident that I could be an amazing mother.

I am a highly educated Black woman spiritual leader, and I have had three abortions throughout my lifetime. There is no way on God's green earth that I would be where I am if I hadn't made the decisions I felt were best for **me** at the time. And, each time, I was deserving and worthy of empathy and grace. So are all women. God cares for us and loves us, regardless of the stigma attached to our choices.

For many women, choosing to have an abortion is extremely sobering. And every woman who decides to terminate her pregnancy deserves the deepest compassion and the safest procedure possible. Any woman who is living a full life post-abortion should not be shamed.

Take a deep inhale, give a full exhale, and breathe this in: Shame does not come from God; shame comes from people. So learn to trust what God says about you and what your body is saying to you.

Listen to Your Body, Sis

Your body is *always* speaking to you! That moment you turn off your alarm and sleep for two more hours is your body crying out for deep rest and restoration. That lingering dull

* Dr. Handy is a womanist, African-centered spiritual leader. She serves as assistant provost at the Interdenominational Theological Center and founding pastor of Rize Community Church, both in Atlanta.

pain that intensifies into a piercing scream is your body nudging you to go to a doctor or holistic practitioner. That eerie suspicion that something is "not quite right" is your intuition telling you, "You in danger, girl!"

Relentlessly exerting energy to run-and-do leaves us very little time to rest-and-be. Constantly rushing to and fro disconnects us from the quiet solitude our minds need to recover, and our bodies need to recharge. Many of us don't like being still for long periods of time, because when we are quiet, our "guck" comes up. But if it's coming up, it needs to come out. James Baldwin wrote, "Not everything that is faced can be changed. But nothing can be changed until it is faced."[3]

After all, energy doesn't dissipate. . . . It transforms. So, we have to be mindful of all the ways our culture urges us to clog the drains of our emotional release. When it comes to grief, we must honor our bodies' truth by being real about what we're feeling—and the truth is not always quiet. Why do we label the processing of pain as "sobbing uncontrollably"? When do we ever sob "controllably"? If it's controlled, it's not sobbing. It's stuffing.

The same way we deserve to reframe our language around God-talk, we also have a right to reframe our language around grief and our bodies' responses to it. In the West, we don't properly give grief the space it needs to *be*. Grief is not something you control; grief is a process you embody.

Grief is not polite, either. It does not gracefully play along with respectability politics. Grief demands attention. Grief yells, then goes silent. Grief is not linear. Sure, researchers have determined that there are five stages of grief, but those are the stages we can quantify. For those of us who have sixth, seventh, and umpteenth stages of grief, our emotions are not processed in a straightforward fashion. There are in-between, liminal spaces that we inhabit. Everybody is different. . . . Every *body* is different.

There is no blueprint for healing after grieving. I haven't had a lot of experience with grief in the traditional death, dying, and bereavement sense. In fact, I used to brag about not being acquainted with grief. My family members have been blessed with long lives. My paternal grandfather was eighty-six years old when he passed away—and that was after he smoked cigarettes for fifty-three years and eventually succumbed to lung cancer. This kind of loss isn't typically considered tragic, because he was up in age. But what about unexpected death? What about unexpected losses that don't *include* death? I would like to see us create pockets of sacred space for those of us who grieve casualties that are unrelated to physical death. "Death" can mean the end of anything: a life, a job, a school, a relationship. But my spiritual belief system includes the idea that the death of one thing is the birth of something else.

Looking for Love

Dating in the Bay Area was a hot mess. I met Hoteps in Oakland, tech bros in San Francisco, and "oh, nos" in Vallejo. I finally joined OkCupid so that I could meet a man who could potentially be my husband. I was particularly enamored with Anthony. He was 6'6", chocolate, with shoulder-length locs and a megawatt smile. He was thirty-five, in finance, and owned a condo and a BMW. Girl . . . I KNOW. The one tiny challenge was that he lived in Washington, DC.

When we first connected, our communication was consistent and compelling for a few days, and then became more infrequent.

"You've been a little quiet lately. . . . Is everything ok?" I inquired.

"Look, Lyvonne. If you were here [in DC], I would be all over you. But I'm just not interested in starting a long-distance relationship right now," he explained.

I had just started a new role as an assistant pastor at a church in Vallejo and it was assumed that I would be there for at least three to five years. Neither Anthony nor I was in a position to move across country, so he thought it would be wise for us to close our romantic chapter. Jesus, Mary, and Joseph! This man wanted commitment and was actually *looking* for a wife and life partner. Talk about bad timing! Don't you just hate it when you meet someone compelling, but the circumstances aren't quite ideal? I know it sucks in the moment, but those are often supernatural prods to let us know that we are on the right path and something better and more aligned is coming.

I was disappointed, but I appreciated his honesty. And, I figured, if *I* wanted to find a husband, I had better look closer to home. I changed my location search settings in the app from "anywhere" to "within 500 miles." That slight adjustment led me to Brandon. Reading his profile felt like I was reading my own. He was into young adult ministry, music, art, and pizza. He had lovely cascading "Brother locs" (I had a thing for locs, chile. I even had my own set at the time) and impeccable, gentlemanly style. There was a quiet elegance about him that intrigued me.

I sent the first message and he took it from there (is intentionality sexy to you, too, Sis?). He confirmed a good time to call and my phone rang right at 9:00 P.M. We talked for three hours, until he asked to FaceTime me. At around midnight we FaceTimed for two more hours and, after that, we were inseparable. We were official within five days (without ever having met in person), living together within three months (he moved from Los Angeles to be with me in the Bay), engaged seven months later, and married nine months after that. WHEW, chile.

Our relationship moved at lightning-fast speed because we both felt like the other person had what we were looking for. Over time, though, we discovered that who we were authentically was not a good match. When it was good, it was GOOD. Until it wasn't.

It started with tiny spats, then shifted to constant bickering, and finally, full-on shouting matches. It got to the point that there were more bad days than good, and that's when I refused to be miserably married for the rest of my life. It was just before our two-year anniversary when I filed for divorce. While I knew it was the best decision for me, it didn't change the fact that I had to honor the stark, grim reality that I was losing the person I thought would be my life partner. Losing the plans I had: to cheer him on at his graduation from Howard University, the $250,000 Atlanta home we wanted to buy, our future son (Caleb) and our future daughter (Parker) whom *he* had chosen names for. None of that would ever come to be in this earthly realm. I didn't just grieve our separation, I grieved the life I lost as a wife and mother.

One afternoon, I was washing dishes in the Oakland apartment we were about to vacate when a wave of anguish came over me. I propped my weight on my forearms, leaned onto the counter, and sobbed. It occurred to me, in that moment, that this was the last time I would ever wash dishes in this apartment. As my tears mixed with running water, suds, and sorrow commingling down the drain, the devastation I felt was insuppressible.

Embodying Grief

Through this experience, I learned that grief is an emotion that must be embodied in order to be processed. Your only role is to discern who you can invite to walk alongside you on your grief journey. Your body knows what to do; all you need is the courage to lean in. There will be days when you don't think it's possible for your tear ducts to produce another single drop, only for the floodgates to open. There will be nights when you disrupt the even inhale-exhale flow of your breath and you choke on your despair. There will be moments when you feel like you will die . . . but you WON'T. Grief teaches us to hold ON.

If you can make it through grief, you can make it through anything. The beauty of embodying grief is that if you allow yourself to feel it, you *will* heal it. We cannot heal from what we are not willing to sit with and allow to wash over us. Grief comes in waves; it ebbs and flows like the tides. Your journey is to surf the emotional swell.

Blogger Jamie Anderson upholds, "Grief, I've learned, is really just love. It's all the love you want to give, but cannot. All that unspent love gathers up in the corners of your eyes, the lump in your throat, and in that hollow part of your chest. Grief is just love with no place to go."[4] A huge part of why I'm able to heal as quickly and holistically as I do is because I give my grief someplace to go. I grieve for fun. I know that may not *sound* fun, but I pounce on any opportunity to grieve. If I'm leading a worship service and I feel the burdens of my congregation, I let the tears fall. If I'm researching my lineage and I sense the somberness of my ancestors, I wail. If I'm scrolling through social media and I see *another* pregnancy or birth announcement, I wince.

Whenever, wherever, if grief shows up, I pay attention to her. In fact, I *expect* her to show up in each and every one of my therapy appointments. If I don't holler, I wonder if I did "the work" during that session. Similarly, I invite you to tap into spaces where you can purge and process without being judged. Be as open and honest as you can so that you can receive the support you richly deserve for your grief journey. Perhaps you need to mute your newly engaged best friend on social media or politely decline the invitation to your former college roommate's baby shower. Listen to your body and then curate your life (digital and analog) in such a way that you support where you are right now, not where you hope to be "one day." The path to regret is paved with "somedays."

Grief visits to allow us to release and transmit the heavy energetic load we may be carrying. Grief is permission to process. In ancient Hebrew times, grieving families were provided food and care for two whole weeks! In modernity, some cultures invite professional mourners to their loved ones' funerals. YES, there are people whose job it is to help induce mourning. It is quite telling that we in the West need grief doulas to help us face the loss, death, and transition of a loved one. If we are still decolonizing grieving death, then we *definitely* need to decolonize non-death-related losses.

Grieving is an inherently embodied experience that takes us on a somatic journey. Somatic healing is focused on getting us into our bodies to help us process our trauma. I am enamored with the idea that there is an entire field of study dedicated to helping us do this, and I like how the *Psychology Today* website frames it:

> Somatic therapy is a form of body-centered therapy that looks at the connection of mind and body and uses both psychotherapy and physical therapies for holistic healing. In addition to talk therapy, somatic therapy practitioners use mind-body exercises and other physical techniques to help release the pent-up tension that is negatively affecting your physical and emotional wellbeing.[5]

We have spent so much time hating, demonizing, and dissociating from our bodies, when, this entire time, it's getting *into* our bodies that brings us salvation. Now is the perfect time to reclaim our bodies as sacred sites of liberation where we experience freedom and safety. The Bible says, "Weeping may linger for the night, but joy comes with the morning."[6] I don't take that to mean that if we lament all night long, when the clock chimes at midnight or when the sun rises at 6:00 A.M., we will be instantaneously whole. Joy does not always come with the morning. No, joy comes with the *mourning*. If you invite grief across the threshold and into your home, joy will come alongside it. If you take a deep dive into your pain, comfort will be there waiting. If you allow yourself to go into the center of your suffering, beloved one, rejoicing will meet you there. Weeping may linger for the night, but joy comes with the MOURNING!

> NO, JOY COMES WITH THE MOURNING.

If we are brave enough to gather the fragmented parts of ourselves, then our God, our ancestors, and our community will help to put us back together again. We become a beautiful mosaic of strength and resiliency as we shift our energy and evolve our lives.

Many of us are cupping grief in our palms when we need to be baptizing ourselves in it. Our bodies have been relegated as sexual entities that we are constantly trying to restrict, but it's time for our bodies to be treated like temples for which others genuflect. You must choose yourself over and over again if you are ever going to feel at home in your body. You must honor the truth of your emotions. It's ok to be not ok. It's *not* ok to be not ok but pretend to be ok.

Toxic positivity is a real thing. Every day is not "good vibes only." Every moment is not always "love and light." We need something for *every* body, *every* emotion, *every* journey. There are some Christian spaces that talk more about Jesus' woundedness than his wholeness. I choose to be made whole. There are some communities of faith who dwell more on his death than his life. I choose life and life more abundantly. An abundant life is a dream-filled life. A life full of pleasure, flow, ease, beauty, wonder, and inspiration!

You are welcome to dream, beloved. After all, I've still got those onesies hanging in my closet in between my "maternity" dresses. So . . . what's in your closet?

Reflect:

He heals the broken-hearted, and binds up their wounds. (Psalm 147:3)

Celebrate:

As you deepen your spiritual practices, remind yourself that healing is:

1. A choice. What's one way that you can choose healing this week? It can be as small or as large as you have the capacity to hold. It just needs to be intentional.
2. A process. Where are you on your journey? Just starting out? Getting warmed up? Deep on your path? Wherever you are, honor it as holy.
3. Not linear. There are five or more stages of grief. You are entitled to feel how you're feeling. Remind yourself that, in the words of wellness coach and radical softness advocate Josh Odam, "the only way through it is through it."

Affirm:

I honor my truth, especially when it comes to pain.
I am worthy of healing.
I am whole.

Chapter 7

Pleasure Is Your Birthright

Curating a Lavish Life of Flow and Ease

"You are not a B student! You are an A student!!!" My father flailed my exam paper wildly in the air as he reprimanded me. My offense? I scored an 83% on a social studies test. I was in the third grade.

As the daughter of Caribbean immigrants, I was raised in a family system that fostered achievement-based worthiness. I felt that I was loved and accepted as long as I was successful. I learned that day that not studying was not an option, and that I had better be a flawless student going forward.

From then on, I got good grades. I was valedictorian in sixth grade and did all the "right" things. And *still* I graduated from college without a job.

Many of us have been in a relentless pursuit of perfection since childhood. By the time I was eleven years old, I had perfected my role as a model student. I got straight As (well, Es for "excellent") and never talked during class—unless I was racing to answer a question. It wasn't unusual for my hand to zip high in the air as my teacher barely finished mouthing her last syllable. I was a board-certified serial-Dean's-List student. School was where I found comfort.

I needed to be perfect: the perfect student, the perfect acolyte, the perfect daughter. While I got good at performing perfection, acting as if I were "perfect" was *exhausting*. And I know I am not an anomaly. Black women are the most educated, highly degreed demographic[1] and the fastest growing population of entrepreneurs.[2] Yet while we are leading the way statistically in education and business, we are still suffering under the weight of a racialized pay gap[3] and other economic inequities.[4,5] A higher percentage of Black women than white women suffer from HIV/AIDS,[6] heart disease,[7] breast cancer,[8] fibroids,[9] and diabetes.[10] Black maternal and infant mortality rates are quadruple the national average of our white counterparts'.[11] Black women's bodies *been* stressed even as we don our Sunday best while toting notebooks emblazoned with "too blessed to be stressed." We stressed, Sis!

The high level of achievement that many laud as "Black Girl Magic"* minimizes the very real physical labor exerted by Black women. Deeply embedded trauma is often teeming just below the surface of our hyper-achievement. There is an explicit connection between being raised in a culture that solely values what we produce and our super-high rates of productivity. Are you *really* on your grind, Sis? Or were you emotionally conditioned to hyper-achieve because you were

---

* This popular hashtag turned phrase and movement was inspired by CaShawn Thompson in 2013.

raised in a merit-based worthiness system—and you feel like you are not worthy to receive love unless you're accomplishing something?

Are you really "busy"? Or are you running? Do you really "work well under pressure" or are you socialized to ramp up your performance while enduring a lot of stress? Are you surviving and calling it thriving because you're doing it all while under duress? Stop and breathe. You are worthy of rest. Rest is healing, and healing is a prerequisite for curating a lavish life of pleasure, flow, ease, and abundance (in ALL of its forms). Leading a life of flow has nothing to do with what you do, and everything to do with *why* you do.

> **LEADING A LIFE OF FLOW HAS NOTHING TO DO WITH WHAT YOU DO, AND EVERYTHING TO DO WITH *WHY* YOU DO.**

All of your degrees and accolades are not the summation of your worth. You are *inherently* worthy because you were born. You do not have to *do* anything to be worthy of love, joy, and rest. These are your birthrights—whether or not anyone ever said you were part of the "Talented Tenth."* You are unique, but you do not need to drive yourself to the point of exhaustion in order to prove it. Burnout is not a bragging right. Exhaustion is not a badge of honor. Think about all the rest your ancestors were *not* allowed to take. Go get theirs, with tax, *plus* interest!

I once called my paternal grandmother and she answered in her typical Guyanese lilt, "Good evening . . . Briggses'!"

"Hey, Granny! How you doing?"

"Hi, Lyvonne! I'm well. . . . How are you doing?"

"I'm good. Just on my grind."

---

* "The Talented Tenth," an idea popularized by thought leader W.E.B. Du Bois, referred to the "tithe" of Black men who, with proper education and training, would be considered worthy leaders for the race.

"What is this 'grind' you speak of? You don't grind. You're not a machine!"

And I oop! Granny read me my rights and Tricia Hersey (aka the Nap Bishop) of the Nap Ministry agrees, "Cancel grind culture." Grinding is not a natural rhythm. Machines grind. Tools grind. Humans cannot grind. Author and entrepreneur Romal Tune says, "Grind is resistance. . . . It's pressure." We disintegrate under that kind of unrelenting tension. Emotional breakdowns happen when we ignore what our bodies are trying to tell us. We're convincing ourselves that we are "making it" when, in reality, we are faking it.

Feel Your Way Through

Audre Lorde, womanist writer and poet (and a beloved ancestor with whom I share Bajan heritage), said in her book *Conversations with Audre Lorde,* "Our feelings are our most genuine paths to knowledge."[12] What you feel is how you know what you need. Many Black women are so consumed with knowing, cerebrally, that they ignore their inner knowing—their gut, their intuition, their guide. The only way to connect with her is to . . . connect with her! Your inner voice and dialogue are of the utmost importance. Your interior life should drip with compassion and kindness. If your inner monologue sounds like a condescending bully, something is out of balance. Don't get me wrong—I'm a Leo sun, Pisces moon, and Leo rising. I'm ambitious. *And* there is a difference between internal motivation and self-imposed obligations that stem from feeling like we are only worthy of love if we are striving for something. When we don't believe that we are inherently worthy, we attempt to make up for our perceived lack with actions. Family, church, and society have saddled us with weight that has tipped the scales of our spiritual, mental, and physical balances. It is time for Black women to rise up from the martyr's altar of people-pleasing.

One scam of epic proportion is the notion of "Black excellence." Black excellence purports that Black people are excellent when we accomplish and produce. Black excellence is a hoax. It is more than a cute catchphrase; it is a repressive ideology and phantom theory that equates our worth to our material achievements and our proximity to whiteness. It is a dehumanizing trope that invokes anxiety and terror in Black bodies. The pressure to be "young, gifted, and Black"[13] is too much! Many of us were raised with the false admonition that "you have to be twice as good to get half as far." Stop it. We are literal geniuses. Living legends. Incarnated icons. Divine beings who are a part of a sacred legacy, who twirl on misogynoir on a daily basis.

"Black excellence" reeks of intracommunal discrimination like colorism, classism, and elitism. All of these systems interlock to create the illusion that we are only as worthy as our bank account or the car we drive. It leaves you running on empty trying to prove your worth by undoing yourself, rushing to accomplish the next thing. When do you rest? When do you go to therapy? When do you masturbate? When do you dream, sleep, move? Eat, pray, love? Laugh, cry, be?

Our inherited hurry can be linked to the antebellum South, when our enslaved foremothers were constantly susceptible to the abuse of their overseers. Then, as post-emancipation sharecroppers, their descendants were exploited by unscrupulous landowners. Soon, domestic workers in the next generations could still suffer regular harm at the hands of their wealthy, white employers. In response to this transgenerational mistreatment, Sistas adapted by shrinking themselves to prevent harm and increase their survival rate. Making ourselves smaller became a form of protection from oppressive forces. Tragically, we have internalized this modality as a means to survive in a racist, anti-Black, capitalist society.

I want to invite you to consider something countercultural and investigate why you only feel good about yourself when you do something great. Thriving in a xenophobic society is inherently great. And you are inherently worthy because you are a child of God! When women are weighted with the unnecessary burden and impossible possibility of perfection, it drives us even deeper into unhealthy ways of being.

It's time to heal the parts of ourselves that think we have to *do* something in order to be loved. "The first step of healing is to know what is in need of healing."[14] You can only receive as much pleasure as you have received healing. This is the season to shift from a mindset of achieving to one of receiving. Sistas who are ready to heal must do the inner work to evolve from *doing* to simply *being*. The Black Girl Magic we espouse is actually our humanity. Like Christ, we are both human and divine; and our divinity includes our legacy of ancestral resiliency. You must get to a point, Sis, where you no longer want your existence to be resistance. I am at a place where I know that I am worthy of softness. I no longer create from a place of protest; I create from being planted in pleasure. Prioritizing your peace *is* a spiritual practice. Peace of mind is wealth. Jesus said, "Peace I leave with you; my peace I give to you."[15] Peace is a gift. . . . Be open to receive it!

> YOU CAN ONLY RECEIVE AS MUCH PLEASURE AS YOU HAVE RECEIVED HEALING.

Receiving, for Black women, is a learning curve. Growing up in church, we were taught that "good girls" are quiet, humble, don't get angry, and are supposed to put all their neighbors before themselves. We learn to "make something out of nothing" when we really should be affirmed as worthy of having our needs met, our desires known, and our wants exceeded. When people want to help you, it does not mean that you are a failure; it means you are worthy of support. In order to truly own our power, we must first learn that accepting help does not mean we are weak, it means we are loved.

> WHEN PEOPLE WANT TO HELP YOU, IT DOES NOT MEAN THAT YOU ARE A FAILURE; IT MEANS YOU ARE WORTHY OF SUPPORT.

Self-awareness is the key to unlocking *why* we feel unworthy. The antidote to unworthiness is a steady diet of divine truths about your personhood and being. Your radical commitment to unapologetic self-love is germinated by reflections and recollections about who—and whose—you are!

If you knew, I mean, *really* KNEW, at a cellular level that you are loved, adored, and cherished, you would make different decisions. Your self-talk would be kinder and you would stunt harder. I know we were raised to be humble, but humility is **not** a divine trait. Yes, the Bible talks about humility, but it's more about avoiding being arrogant and looking down on other people. Even still, have you ever looked up the word "humble"? According to Dictionary.com it's:

> having a feeling of insignificance, inferiority, subservience, etc.
> low in rank, importance, status, quality, etc.
> low in height, level, etc.; small in size

Um. . . . No, sir! No, ma'am! No, gender nonconforming folx! I am NOT humble, and you shouldn't be, either. Colonized religion taught us that humility is a godly attribute, but what about God is humble? After God created the world,

God's Self said, "It is good." Hun-nee, bay-bee! You are GOOD. And when I say "good," I mean GREAT. I mean beautiful, bountiful, lacking nothing. Screw being humble! Stunt. On. Us!

Take Up Space, Sis

The very fact that you desire something is evidence that you deserve it. In the words of affirmation musician and song-writer Toni Jones, "Take Up Space, Sis." The religion of my childhood taught me to beg God for my blessings. The faith of my adulthood empowers me to claim my birthright! You are worthy. There is nothing you want that is out of reach for you.

Now, listen: I'm talking about *your* purpose and your *calling*. I'm not talking about someone else's husband. You will come to know that, as long as your desire is ethical and aligned, nothing is too good for you. . . . No *thing* is too good for you! The implications of Black women knowing that they are deserving of God's best are robust.

Some of us were raised in traditions that forbade girls and women from wearing pants, lipstick, earrings, or any hairstyle more opulent than a simple ponytail. Pentecostal, apostolic, and holiness denominations trained us to down-play our beauty. You know—1 Timothy 2:9 it up. Be modest. No gold, no pearls. But when Paul was writing to Timothy, he was talking about women who were so flashy that they were distracting from the growth of the church; women who brought attention to themselves by showing off their wealth (and thinking that their affluence made them better than other people). He was not talking about women who are simply adorning their bodies as an act of lavish self-care.

Self-care is not just a cute phrase, it is a moral obligation.

It is more than trips to luxury day spas and sipping champagne at fancy nail salons. While all that is nice, care of the body is, in fact, care for the soul. Love is not a concept, it is a verb. Love of self is an evolution. My prayer for you is that you nurture yourself along a path of unfolding to self-awareness, self-compassion, and self-worth.

I invite you to engage a radical ethic: Who we are is enough, and we do not have to achieve our way to worthiness. If you are apprehensive, dear one, I understand. Move at your own pace as you begin or deepen your practice of pleasure. My dear Sista-friend, writer and poet Rev. Hazel M. Cherry, identifies pleasure as a fruit of the Spirit, and I pray this concept empowers you to embrace your sensuality.

> CARE OF THE BODY
> IS, IN FACT,
> CARE FOR THE SOUL.

When the chaotic pace of capitalism attempts to disrupt my enjoyment stream, I disrupt it right back. Every day, multiple times a day, I ask myself, *What would bring me joy right now?* And then, to the extent that it's possible, I do that. This is a revolutionary framework for actively and consistently inviting pleasure into my life. Our pleasure is our responsibility. What is one way you can invite pleasure into your life today? Is it a nap? A scoop of nondairy ice cream? FaceTiming your person? A clearance candle from Ross? Pause for a moment, close your eyes (if you feel comfortable), take a deep, cleansing breath, and tap into what simple act would bring you pleasure in the next twenty-four to forty-eight hours. And make it *happen*!

You might be thinking, *But, Lyvonne . . . I don't have* time *for all that!* You *do* have the time, beloved—you're just not prioritizing yourself. Checking in with your joy level is more than a routine. It's a ritual. To this day, there are still moments when I have to remind myself that who I am is enough—that I do not have to *do* anything in order to be pampered or spoiled. Who I am, as a child of God, a human being, and a resident of planet Earth, is ENOUGH.

When God said, "Let there be," there was. That means everything you want already is. So, all you have to do is *be*. Giving deep thought to what brings you joy in your body will inevitably lead you to consider every other part of your life. When you ask, "What brings me joy?" you'll begin to question *everything*. Is this romantic relationship still serving me? This job? This belief system? This narrative I keep retelling myself? There is no way to change without focusing on yourself. And we have been told that caring for ourselves is selfish; so who, then, is caring for us?

Warped Legacy of Work

In 1918, the city of Greenville, South Carolina, tried to force Black women to work. In a *Greenville News* article entitled "Negro Women to Be Put to Work," the City Council introduced an ordinance that "Regardless of whether they want to or have to, able bodied negro women in Greenville who are not regularly employed are to be put to work, put in jail or fined heavily."[16] Black wives who were financially supported by their working husbands and did not have to work provided a shortage of "cooks and laundresses" for white families. Why didn't poor white women take these domestic jobs? We live in a society with a legacy of people who would rather create laws to force us to labor in their homes than simply hire non-Black women who actually need a job. It's bizarre.

With this kind of warped legacy of work, it's no surprise that Black women are often the most laborious in corporate halls, church sanctuaries, and our home fronts. Do you see why actively resisting working yourself to the point of death is a spiritual practice that gives life to our bloodlines? Lavishing your body-temple with rest and pleasure is proof that you are honoring yourself, your ancestors, *and* God!

Less Work, More Play

"Celebrate always, pray constantly, and give thanks."[17] Get out into nature. Listen to music, admire art, and watch films that inspire you. Creativity is a cosmic tool that enhances a woman's ability to flow. Play is a critical component of creativity. Black women need to play more.

Laughter and pleasure jump-start our imagination. There really is no such thing as an overactive imagination. Your "wild" imagination is a direct connection to Spirit. When you were younger and had an "imaginary friend," that was probably an ancestor or spirit guide.

Likewise, when you're a child, people tell you, "Be creative!" or "Think big!" and "Think outside the box!" But when you're an adult, if you even *think* about stepping your pinky toe outside of the box, the system bucks:

"You can't do that."
"It's never been done before."
"We don't do things that way."

Our great ancestor Nelson Mandela said, "It always seems impossible until it's done."

Beloved, *anything* is possible. If we truly believe that we serve a God that can do anything; if we actually breathe in the Scripture where Jesus says, "The one who believes in me will also do the works that I do and, in fact, will do *greater* works than these";[18] if we finally internalize that we are human expressions of the Divine on the earth, then we will know that there is NOTHING we cannot do. "Nothing will be impossible with God."[19] And don't let anyone tell you otherwise!

Anything that does not bring you joy is not for you. Even the work you do to sustain yourself and your family should bring you joy. You cannot create the life of your dreams without shedding the effects of your nightmares. Taking delicate, intentional steps to feel at home in your body-temple starts with paying attention to her. Pay special attention to tender areas. Centering your constant joy will lead to your ultimate pleasure.

And while pleasure *includes* sex, pleasure is absolutely about *more* than sex. *But sex is reserved for married people!* you might think. If that were the case, then only heterosexual married people would have sexual organs and urges. Am I saying that every sexual urge should be acted upon? Absolutely not. Pedophilia is evil and rape is sin. My sex talk centers grown, consenting, stable adults. Your natural urges are not some ongoing string of battles that you need to "overcome." They are divinely designed unctions that are worthy of exploration within safe, intimate spaces. Just think: All the time and energy you wasted fighting your nature could have been used to embrace joy! It's time to tap in, Sis. Your supreme satisfaction is waiting on you.

Reflect:

The thief comes only to steal and kill and destroy. I came that they may have life, and have it abundantly. (John 10:10)

Celebrate:

Any time is a good time to care for your body. Here are some of my favorite ways to pamper myself:

Take an afternoon nap.

Block off a day to clear out your closet.
Try on everything and sell or donate anything that does not make you feel sexy or regal.

Dance naked in front of the mirror! If you're not quite comfortable baring it all, you can start by dancing in clothes. Bonus points for recording yourself!

Say it loud, say it proud! "Black Pleasure Matters." From luxury vacations to opulent orgasms, you deserve pleasure, beloved one.

Affirm:

Pleasure is my birthright.
I create from ease and pleasure.
Play is the pathway to joy.*

* I first heard this from author and speaker Aarona Leá.

Chapter 8

Masturbation Is a Gift from God

Getting Acquainted with Desire

My older sister gifted me with my very first vibrator when I was nineteen years old. As I slid the case out of a nondescript light brown paper bag, I had no idea what I was holding. The black-and-purple package felt like something powerful and royal, but I was clueless about what to do with this "adult toy."

One night, just before bedtime, I unsealed the box and slid the plastic-wrapped apparatus out of its container. After skimming the instructions, I connected the charger to the port, plugged it into my surge protector, hid the rigged-up device under my bed, and went to sleep. I was certain that when I awoke, the vibrator's indicator light would have turned from a steady red light to a strong green color. I was right! Green meant "go"! Now that it was fully charged, it was time to plot the right time to ... *engage.* After all, I still lived at home with my parents and younger brother, and I was NOT going to have *any* of my relatives walk in on me during my ultra-VIP session.

Eventually, I worked up the nerve to try my vibrator on for size (and function). I lay back on my twin-size bed (did I mention I was still living at home, y'all?), wearing just an oversized T-shirt (the pajama "uniform" of Caribbeans the world over!). I unraveled the long black straps and laced my legs through each one. As I pulled my sensual pet closer to my hips, I could not, for the life of me, figure out the placement for the tiny red plastic hummingbird. It turns out ... it was because I didn't know where my clitoris was.

I placed the hummingbird over my general vaginal area and turned it on. It immediately started bobbing aggressively, and I freaked out. Looking back, I know the settings were turned up way too high, but back then? Oh, honey ... that was all she wrote. I packed that thing up (totally wrong, by the way, because I couldn't even get the box to close properly) and chucked it in a trash can at the Jamaica Center–Parsons/Archer subway station. To this day, I wonder if someone riding the E train happened across this contraption that was supposed to bring me so much pleasure.

If you're anything like nineteen-year-old me, you were totally clueless about your pleasure center. You're not alone. Many of us do not use the anatomically correct names for our sexual organs, much less know where they are and what they do. As Black, churched women, we were never encouraged to get acquainted with our genitalia. We were indoctrinated to believe that our bodies were evil, our sexuality was shameful, and our desire was demonic; and, moreover, that sex was only for men's—correction: our *husbands'*—pleasure.

From the time we are children to the moment we enter adulthood (and throughout our mature years, for some), what we want takes a back seat to what other people want for us. Family, church, and society have all done their respective numbers on our psyches by forcing us to believe that our sexuality (a sacred gift) is something to be repressed and shamed.

Since God made us, that means that God made our sexual desires, too. And since God is good, that means that our sexuality is good, too. Ethical, healthy, safe sexual desires are a normal part of our human experience. And, since we are human expressions of God on the earth, that means that our sexuality is godly. Being a body- and sex-positive pastor means that I no longer fight, resist, or hate the things that my body does "God-given-ly." For decades, I have dishonored my temple by being unkind to myself and demonizing my desires—sensual, sexual, or otherwise. It's exhausting being at odds with yourself. A house divided against itself cannot stand,[1] and I got tired of trying to build my faith on a cracked foundation.

If you're looking to furnish your home with abundant pleasure and radical self-love, reclaiming your sexuality is a great place to start. In order to become the sexual goddess you were born to be, you must first delight in your senses. You want the blueprint to getting comfortable with your sexuality? Pay attention to what tantalizes you. What ignites your desire? And by "desire," I don't mean what you want to eat for breakfast or the salted dark chocolate you crave when you're on your cycle. I mean your *core* desires. What turns you on? What gets you going?

Trust Yo'self

We all have core desires. Each one of us possesses a set of passionate wants that would bring us immense enjoyment. But we can't get to the heart of our core desires if we don't even know what we like. How could you? Your youth pastor was tormenting you with the idea that your "heart is deceitful above all things, and desperately wicked: who can know it?"[2] If your earliest spiritual leaders habituated you not to trust yourself, it's no wonder you don't. Those are the parts of ourselves that we must lean into: What brings you bliss? Do you even know?

Once, I delivered my signature keynote, "The Pleasure Principle," at a conference for Black women in Twin Cities, Minnesota. Afterward, I led a talkback where one of the attendees emphasized my point about knowing what you desire. She recounted that she had made scrambled eggs for her children for so long that when the youngest left for college and she went to cook eggs for herself, she didn't even know how she liked them! Imagine cheffing it up in the kitchen for DECADES for your loved ones only to turn around and, when given ample space and opportunity to cook a luscious, nourishing meal for yourself, you don't even know what you like!

Beloved, you must prepare to receive your preference. You must know that you are so beyond worthy of receiving what you want that you open yourself up to take in all the goodness that wants to flow to you, as seamlessly as your next breath.

Self-Love Is the Best Love

Masturbation is the safest, most consensual sex you can have. Therefore, it makes the best entrée into learning what your sexual desires are. Before you can share what you like with your

> YOU MUST KNOW THAT YOU ARE SO BEYOND WORTHY OF RECEIVING WHAT YOU WANT THAT YOU OPEN YOURSELF UP TO TAKE IN ALL THE GOODNESS THAT WANTS TO FLOW TO YOU, AS SEAMLESSLY AS YOUR NEXT BREATH.

partner (or, let's be real . . . *partners*), you have to be able to indulge in it yourself first. Like Teyana Taylor sang in "Made It," "Self-love is the best love!"

Masturbation is a gift from God. And it is the gift that keeps on giving. Masturbation is also a lot of fun. Exploring your body is the sweetest adventure. Just when you think you've identified all of your erogenous zones, a finger brushes against here or your vibrator touches there and, next thing you know, you've got a dozen new hot spots! DELICIOUS.

Now, if you're like my younger self, you are clutching your pearls just *reading* the word "masturbation." I get it. We were taught to believe that it is bad, evil, and we would go to hell if we touched ourselves. But lemme free you real quick— since I know "Pastor Johnson" of "Ebenezer Bedside Baptist Church of God on Christ the Solid Rock I Stand International Ministries" is not going to let your church have a Masturbation Sunday. There is no way to write about pleasure without talking about solo sexy time, and I'm here to help!

Masturbation has been unnecessarily vilified by those who grossly misinterpret the Bible. The Scripture most Christians point to when they try to adamantly condemn masturbation is Genesis 38:9–10, where a Brotha named Onan "spilled his semen on the ground," which was "displeasing in the sight of the LORD," and so Onan got got!

Y'all really think YHWH* was putting people to death for masturbating? Nah, fam. What had happened was: Onan was the middle son. His older brother, Er, was wicked in Yahweh's sight, so Yahweh killed him. In ancient biblical culture, the oldest brother was supposed to be the inheritor and patriarch-to-be. But, if the eldest brother died childless, the

---

* "LORD" is a translation of "YHWH" (Yahweh) and it means "self-existent."

Old Covenant dictated that the dead brother's next closest single male relative was to procreate with the dead big brother's widow in order to produce an heir. So Onan's dad, Judah, told Onan to have sex with Er's widow (Tamar) so that there would be a firstborn heir to keep the patriarchal lineage going. Whew . . . Y'ALL! Who needs soap operas when you got the Hebrew Bible? The DRAMA! Do you see where I'm going with this? *Leans in and whispers* *They were African!* Israel was Nollywood before Nollywood was Nollywood.

But I digress.

Onan was not here for his semen impregnating a woman who would have a son (we presume) who would get all the rights that come with being the firstborn—while Onan was relegated to second-son citizenship. Onan was petty AF. And probably ashy, too. He refused to ejaculate into his sister-in-law because he knew that he was not going to reap the benefits of fathering that child. Onan was shirking his covenantal duties and *that* (major key alert!) is why Yahweh was angry with him! This Scripture that folks have been abusing for generations to demonize masturbation, and even birth control, has nothing to do with either and everything to do with fulfilling a covenant with God and God's people.

Let this be a liberative moment for you, Sis. There is NO verse in the Bible that condemns masturbation. The "sexual immorality"[3] that people point to in the Pauline epistles also has nothing to do with solo sexy time. It is just that, culturally, we have lumped in any and all sexual activity that is not committed within a heterosexual marriage to be "sinful."

Remember the query of my friend Xan: "Who does it serve for you to believe the text this way?"

Sin is not a legalistic set of dos and don'ts. Pastor Mark A. Lomax says, "Sin is separation from God." So, the fact that we are running from our Creator after engaging in healthy, consensual sexual activity is the sin. The idea that we can't love God and love sex is the sin. The sin is church leaders who learn the truth about our bodies and our sexuality as it relates to Scripture and, instead of teaching their congregations the truth, they perpetuate lies because (as I have heard) "I can't say that in my church." The sin is that we have Black pastors who internalize and reinforce colonized religion that oppresses, rather than uplifts, Black women. *That,* my dear Sista, is the sin!

Use Your Head

If we are ever to repair the breach between the people and the book, we must endeavor to healthily honor the truths of our sacred text. We must venture to create a church where we do not limit God's divinity to the God of the Bible, but rather, we honor that all of our lives are sacred texts. Your lived experiences are holy and true, and no one knows them like God and you. You are the master of your fate and the captain of your soul.* And there is no reason for you to be this incredibly powerful spiritual being who suffers in her flesh for the sake of "holiness." You are holy just by being, so *be.*

Be in your body. Be in your Creation. Be in your goodness. And if you need some seductive suggestions, here are a few to whet your appetite!

Relax

Don't be like me. The first time I attempted to use a vibrator was one of the first times I *ever* tried to masturbate. I was ignorant about my body parts *and* the hummingbird. Do some research with you as the subject. Have you ever seen your vagina? If you need permission to go look at your nether re-

---

* A riff off of William Ernest Henley's poem "Invictus."

gions, please consider this your hall pass. Grab a compact mirror, sit on the toilet or the edge of your bed, spread your legs, and look at your vulva. The Planned Parenthood website includes simple but straightforward definitions:

> The vulva is the part of your genitals on the outside of your body—your labia, clitoris, vaginal opening, and the opening to the urethra (the hole you pee out of). While vaginas are just one part of the vulva, many people say "vagina" when they really mean the vulva. But the vulva has a lot more going on than just the vagina. . . .
>
> The labia (lips) are folds of skin around your vaginal opening. The labia majora (outer lips) are usually fleshy and covered with pubic hair. The labia minora (inner lips) are inside your outer lips.[4]

Then, there's your clitoris, located where the inner lips meet. When you are sexually aroused, one or more of these elements can swell. But your clitoris is like Visa—it's everywhere you want to be. Because while the clitoris looks tiny, looks can be deceiving. Your clitoris has two "legs" that reach five inches inside your body![5] Beloved, the average size of an adult erect penis is five to seven inches long. Your clitoral legs are as long as some men's erect penis and you have *two* of them! That is evidence that women are owed double the amount of sexual pleasure of men. Ladies, we have some MAJOR catching up to do!

I know God created pleasure because God created the clitoris. The clitoris is the only organ on any creature that has one sole, delicious, pleasurable function. Why would God give me something as delectable as a clitoris and then tell me that I can't use it? My God is not a sadomasochist. My God is a God of love and light and liberation.

It can be disconcerting for Christian women to take the first few steps toward sexual self-discovery. I get the trepidation, fear, and shame. *And,* if you start from a place where your body, yes, your vagina, is created in the image and likeness of God, you will soon see your body—*all* of your body—as divine. In fact, "yoni," a term that has been popularized in the women's wellness industry in recent years, is a Sanskrit word meaning "abode, source, womb, or vagina."[6] While colonized Abrahamic religions do not honor the Divine Feminine, there are thousands of world religions that do. For example, Hinduism, an Indian belief system, celebrates the generative power of women. I imagine how little girls who grow up with renderings of God that look like them could grow to embrace their own humanity and celebrate their inherent divinity. Rather than listening to the toxic misogyny that runs rampant in our culture, we would have space to embrace the natural dip of our hips as well as the curve of our lips . . . *all* of them.

We are living in an era where we are reclaiming our bodies, minds, and spirits. I invite you to liberate yourself with your language, first and foremost. Disruptor, healer, and founder of The Alter Call* Dr. Crystal Jones empowered me to shift from using the word "decolonize" to "liberate." Dr. Jones and I were sipping tea (literally *and* figuratively) at Just Add Honey Tea Company in Atlanta, when she casually communicated, "Your cells hear everything." I stopped in my tracks. If you are constantly talking about getting free, but your language is still bound, you are subverting your efforts.

When we say "decolonize," we're still centering colonization. But when we transform our tongue to say "liberate," we are focusing on freedom. We are calling in a creed and culture that compels rather than repels us from engaging our bodies.

---

* The Alter Call offers spiritual mentoring and consulting for individuals ready to heal and reorganize their nervous systems.

Liberate your mind, your language, and your body— in that order! Your vagina is not "nasty." It does not smell "bad." Our vaginas are not supposed to smell like raindrops on roses or tropical mango smoothies. You own a pussy—not a papaya. And if you *do* perceive a pungent stench, that means that something is wrong and you should seek medical care.

Embracing your sexuality is a part of your spirituality. The closer you are to being at home in your body, the closer you are to God. God delights in your pleasure. Don't you think you should, too?

Relate

Create a warm, inviting environment, preferably somewhere private. I was in my parents' home, not a private abode. Plan your self-gratification dates when your family or roommates are away for an extended period of time. Or, make it a lush love date and reserve a room at the fanciest hotel your budget will allow. Soak in a luxurious bath or steam in a shower with a deliciously scented body scrub. I prefer longer soaks in my tub and I finish with manual exfoliation so that my skin is optimally supple. What you want to create is an atmosphere of praise for your flesh.

Release

You are a precious object and you deserve to be lavishly loved. Set up the space the way you would if you were expecting a lover to come over. Go to Ross, HomeGoods, T.J. Maxx, Marshalls, or your favorite shop and buy some sumptuously scented bath salts. Invest in enticing mood lighting. You can light some exquisitely fragranced candles (Ikea's tealights are SUPER affordable!), click on a Himalayan pink salt lamp, or string some fairy lights above your headboard. Play some sultry tunes (I love my Tank Pandora station), put on your favorite robe (or a soft, comfy T-shirt with NO undies), and lie in your bed. The mood is set. You have no one to please except yourself. Take your time and relish each savory moment.

Solo sexy time is a priority for me. It especially helps me through d-droughts. *eggplant emoji* Masturbation will not remove the desire for a partnership. Masturbation will, however, provide opportunities for full-body healing. Masturbating to orgasm releases endorphins, relieves stress, and boosts immunity. Coming literally keeps you going! It's how I know that God intends for masturbation to bring us peace of mind, not internal turmoil. My God is a God of healing, wholeness, and wellness.

The next time you're sexually aroused and shame tries to creep on you, reject it! Remind yourself:

I am a sensual being.
Sexuality is a gift.
I deserve pleasure.
Pleasure is my birthright.

Come back to your breath. Practicing mindfulness brings you back to center and helps you to feel present in the moment. Inhale deeply and exhale fully. You cannot release if you are not relaxed, and you will not relax if you are not breathing. Ease your way into it and offer yourself grace. Be patient and kind, just like you would expect a lover to be with you. You can start by massaging your neck and shoulders, then tracing your fingertips down your stomach. Caress your thighs and really *feel* your body: the bumps and bruises, the scars and scabs, the hair (pubic and ingrown), the dimples and stretch marks.

Try different angles, motions, and even parts of your body, since there are at least eleven different kinds of orgasms.[7] Now before you try to go from zero to a hundred real quick, let's start with four.

Clitoral

You stimulate your clitoris (and the areas around it) with your fingers or a vibrator. There are eight thousand nerve endings in the clitoris, double the number that are in the penis.[8] If someone is getting on your last nerve, they should get on one of those.

Vaginal

Your fingers, hands, or a toy are all great for vaginal stimulation. Start with gentle massaging before moving on to different motions that feel good to you. Circles, in-and-out, or a mix of both could be just what your vagina ordered.

Anal

You might think your booty hole is off-limits, but it's anything *butt*. After a succulent soak or shower, you can feel free to explore the erogenous zones lying underneath your cheeks. You can use anal toys and plugs to climax. With our booties, we can twerk one minute and orgasm the next!

Combo

Ok, so this one does not come with fries and a drink, but it *can* be supersized! You can intensify your pleasure by arousing two or more of your erogenous zones simultaneously.

How are you holding up, Sis? That was a lot, I know. But the most beautiful part of this work is that you do not have to stir up any of this before you are ready.[9] You have agency and you get to unfold to this journey on your own time at your own pace. Like grief, healing is not linear, and you may find yourself bouncing back and forth between points and vacillating between total comfort and utter dismay. And guess what? That's ok.

Your goal is to express what feels good to you in your own divine timing. All the articles, books, webinars, seminars, retreats, and coaching in the world will not aid you if you do not sit with, and internalize, the fact that all of this body-talk is your immaculate inheritance. God does not want you at war with your body. We must end the deification of suffering. In the words of Pastor Kanyere Eaton, "God is not glorified by your chronic exhaustion." Your weariness from being at war with your body does not serve God and it does NOT serve you. You are worthy of pleasure. Pleasure is your birthright.

Invest in Social Currency

If you're still getting stuck in your head, however, get into your body. The more in touch you are with your body, the more in *touch* you are with yourself! Tap in with like-minded people who are open to nuanced, holistic conversations about religion and sexuality. Follow people who inspire you regarding faith and sex. Pay attention to the comment section on their posts. Don't be afraid to shoot your platonic shot in the name of finding community. You will be surprised who you will align with when you begin to uncover your intimate thoughts and questions. When you allow yourself to be open (with discernment), God will honor your vulnerability.

To get started, I would suggest following a mix of people who are liberating Christianity, fostering self-love, inspiring your creative juices, and some who are eye candy. Discover KIMBRITIVE[10] on social media and join the Black Women Deserve Great Sex™ movement. Black women owning our sexual pleasure is a revolution. Why not make the revolution sumptuous? In *Conversations with Toni Cade Bambara,* Bambara espouses, "As a cultural worker who belongs to an oppressed people my job is to make revolution irresistible."[11] What's more alluring than a faith-filled woman who embraces her sensuality, owns her sexuality, and loves herself unapologetically?

Loving yourself without apology requires self-delight. You must be able to take in and love all the parts of yourself that others might deem unacceptable. The unsavory parts of yourself that you would rather hide than amplify. We all have things about ourselves that we don't talk about during the job interview or on the first date. But what if we could look at and identify those parts of ourselves and bring even more grace and compassion to them? What if we trusted that if God can love all of you, then you can love all of you, too? When we shift from seeing ourselves as inherently evil beings to blessed creatures of God, we can encounter life as a string of experiences rather than a series of tests.

We don't have anything to prove to God, only to other people. But when you know you are enough simply because you are beloved of God, you grow to realize that you do not need any external validation; you will start to put your needs first. It is time for Black Christian women to make themselves not sinful wretches, but the main characters in our lives. We get to—like God does—create, rest, dream, and wonder as a part of our holy heritage. We get to play and learn and grow by using our senses to encounter the world. And when we take on a sense of wonder, we have more fun. And what's more pleasing

> WHEN WE SHIFT FROM SEEING OURSELVES AS INHERENTLY EVIL BEINGS TO BLESSED CREATURES OF GOD, WE CAN ENCOUNTER LIFE AS A STRING OF EXPERIENCES RATHER THAN A SERIES OF TESTS.

than fun?! Pleasure is your birthright, beloved, and sensuality is your claim ticket. Being in your body demands that the Divine meet you wherever you are along your journey.

Now, while God is ever present for your spiritual, sensual, and sexual growth, not everyone is here for your total healing. The function of patriarchy is to beguile women into deepening our self-doubt and hollowing our agency. Society does not know what to do with liberated women. In fact, history shows us that they fear us. I say we scare the hell out of 'em, Sis! I mean, if sex is so bad, why do we sometimes shout "Oh, God!" when we come? Orgasms are spiritual experiences and they build our connections to ourselves and to God. The body-soul connection is powerful beyond measure and deserves to be handled with care.

Sadly, capitalism "prowls around, looking for someone to devour."[12] The billion-dollar beauty industry does not profit off women who love themselves, and neither does the church. If these institutions can keep us running in circles, at odds with our divine sexual nature, we will more likely acquiesce in the proposed "solutions" they posit. It may not be New Year's, but now is the perfect time to come up with resolutions that feel good to *you*.

Just think of all the heartache you could have avoided if, instead of texting that dusty miscreant at 2:00 A.M., you had rubbed one out. Or, rather than staying with your toxic ex way beyond your relationship's expiration date because the sex was good, you invested in toys that could bring you similar (if not better!) sexual pleasure. The orgasm gap[13] is real and it's time we close it.

Our Pleasure Matters

As a womanist, I center Black women's pleasure and I am infuriated when people convert Genesis 38 to an ode against

masturbation because they are essentially erasing Tamar.*
What's the story from this Sista's point of view? Imagine this:
You are grieving the death of your husband when you receive
word that, due to your religious law, you must procreate with
the brother-in-law in order to give birth to the son you were
supposed to have with the now-dead love of your life. Rather
than grieving fully and transitioning to life as a widow, you
are forced to have sex with a man who repeatedly ejaculates
onto the ground instead of into you. Might you be wondering, *What's wrong with me?* Worst of all, if the sexual acts are
against your will, that means the sex is not consensual. And
there's no such thing as "nonconsensual sex"; that is rape. So
you endure the sexual assault to get pregnant and the one
thing you need to conceive a child is being wasted on the
ground. How maddening! But folks want to talk about "masturbation." TUH. From now on, I will honor Tamar by being
in my body on my own terms. I will luxuriate in the everyday.

Inviting sexual power into your daily life begins with cul-
tivating sensual arousal. You are a spiritual being having a
physical experience. Engage your senses. Delight in worldly
wonder. You can enjoy sex. Women get to enjoy sex, too! You
deserve big, bodacious, blessed orgasms. And masturbation
is the gift that will get you there.

Whenever you are in a sexy mood, remind yourself that
the Bible does not condemn masturbation. Sexual activity is
not inherently immoral, and masturbation is the gift from
God that keeps on coming and giving at the same damn time.
So let's get closer to God, one orgasm at a time!

* This Tamar in Genesis 38 is not the Tamar from 2 Samuel 13 nor the
Braxtons.

Reflect:

If the Son makes you free, you will be free indeed. (John 8:36)

Celebrate:

Self-Care: Liberating desire is critical for the Sensual Faith initiate. You must excavate and uncover your core desires. Rather than hold fast to what was ingrained in you, you get to explore what really gets you going. Set aside an afternoon to journal and ponder:

What made you happy as a child? What makes you happy as an adult? Where is the overlap? What brings you joy these days? What does your daily rhythm feel like? What would your ideal daily rhythm feel like? Compare the lists and intentionally pursue each of those things to the extent that they are possible.

Community Care: The next time you're kiki'ing with your girls, ask them if they masturbate. Depending on who you're with, you might be able to foster a dialogue with your inner circle. Assess each individual's comfort level with the conversation alongside the group's dynamic. As you begin to have public-facing talks about sex, you will quickly realize how polarizing it is. There will be women who are excited and ready to talk about their favorite positions and sex toys and there will be some who think sex talk is crude and shouldn't be discussed openly. However, if you want to truly engage this Sensual Faith journey, you will need community. You will want to share articles and tweets and TikToks and Instagram Reels and you don't need someone clobbering you with Bible verses and guilt. Who can you have these daring discussions with?

Who is equipped to be a part of the group chat? You will want to be sure that they can hold and share brave space with you because this is an ongoing dialogue that requires nuance and care. You are worthy of a healing, fully integrated, aligned community!

Affirm:

I am a sensual being.
I deserve pleasure.
My desires matter.

Chapter 9

Beautiful Scars

Re-membering to Love Yourself Unapologetically

I sat perched on the toilet, wincing, and doubled over in pain. For days, every time I peed, I felt like someone was raking hot coals across my vulva. It was so bad that I started peeing standing up in the shower just to simply soothe the burning sensations. The pain was enough to make me dehydrate myself just so I could lessen the frequency with which I had to urinate . . . *not* healthy. I assumed I had a UTI (urinary tract infection) and so that Sunday after church, I asked my Sista-friend Estee what I should do. She was our friend group's resident sexologist and usually offered solid advice.

"I think I have a urinary tract infection. . . . What should I do?" I inquired.

"Vitamin C, cranberry juice, drink lots of water, and you can try some Azo," she offered.

Azo, I made a mental note. *Got it.*

I Googled "Azo" and read some of the reviews so I was optimistic about healing my condition. I went to a local convenience store, purchased a box (extra strength!), and headed home to ingest these medicinal tablets. I took a few doses of the Azo for a couple of days, but my symptoms didn't improve.

I decided to make an appointment to see a doctor at the Feminist Women's Health Center in Atlanta. The center was stale and stoic, but, hey, it offered accessible medical care. And, as I was uninsured and paying out of pocket, I needed to make it do what it do. The front-desk attendant was aloof, but I didn't have the energy to try to engage her. *I* was the one who needed care in that moment. I politely informed her that I was there for a 7-panel STD screening test, and I paid my fee. I was the only person in the waiting area so the technician was able to get to me quickly. She drew a few vials of my blood, bandaged me up, and sent me on my way.

I had expected to receive a physical examination with my screening, but it turns out, that was a totally separate service. So, I went *back* to the front desk and asked the attendant if I could see the nurse on duty. As she took my payment for the in-person visit, she called over her shoulder, "She wants to see someone." And the two women behind her rolled their eyes and exhaled loudly.

I was utterly confused as to why women servicing women at a place called the *Feminist* Women's Health Center could be so callous. But my emotional capacity to navigate other people's irritation was nonexistent in that moment.

One of the women called me to the back, led me to an examination room, and gave me a paper skirt to change into. A few minutes later, when the attending nurse came in, I noted how young she looked in her basic Banana Republic sweater and jeans. Where were her scrubs? Her white lab coat? Apparently, she was a *student* nurse at nearby Emory University who was getting her practice hours in, which was not an excuse but it helped me understand why her bedside manner was so horrendous.

She examined me and informed me that I had contracted genital herpes. I remember lying on the examination table and sobbing, "I can't believe this! I always tell my students 'no glove, no love' and now look at me!" I was distraught. I thought my life was over. Thanks to the stigma and shame attached to sexually transmitted diseases and infections, I thought that I was "gross" and "dirty." The narrative I created in my head was that I would never find love because, *Who would want me* now?

As I processed all this in real time, the practicing nurse looked irritated. She did not console me with statistics nor did she offer me an initial care plan.

I also felt defeated because I always made it a point to initiate a sexual wellness talk with any potential partner. But just *talking* about safe sex is not safe sex. And even if we were super careful in the beginning (down to my carrying my own condoms), at some point in my exclusive, committed relationships, we would default to sex without protection. Despite knowing better, I also had unprotected sex with men I was *not* in a committed relationship with.

In fact, I had a hunch about who I contracted the virus from, and we weren't together at that time. But I was not 100% certain because herpes is a virus that can lie dormant in your body until something activates it. So, I could have contracted it from a partner *years* prior and simply didn't know because I was leading a mellow life. But, baby, life be lifing and, for me, I was in a high-stress season and that's what activated the virus in my body.

I was planning to move across the country for a full-time

pastoral role and it was SUPER intense for me. I remember running around trying to say goodbye to all of my Atlanta friends, selling my car, shipping my belongings, and still dating through it all.

It was a LOT. And it didn't stop there. Once I relocated to California, I had my *second* outbreak a month later. Stress is a major trigger that reactivates the herpetic virus. I didn't have sex for months after that. But, when Brandon and I started dating, he revealed something to me that made me feel like he was a keeper.

Remember the first marathon phone call I mentioned? Well, the conversation was easy, organic, and fluid until . . . he paused. "I want to be completely honest with you from the beginning," he segued. I braced myself.

"I contracted genital herpes," he disclosed steadily.

My tummy deflated. It was like a sonic vacuum sucked the life force from my voice box.

"Hello?" he prodded gently. Later on, he confessed that he'd thought, in that moment, he had lost me. But I managed to shake off how stunned I was and finally uttered:

"Me, too."

What a relief to meet someone who knew what it was like to live with a sexually transmitted disease and did not wait for ME to bring it up! It was one of the more honorable things I admired about him. Especially because in our culture and on social media, we tend to stigmatize, shame, and make fun of people living with herpes. About 25% of the American population has herpes and many don't even know it.[1] This is why we should aim to be more upfront about our sexual health and consider making getting tested a biannual spiritual practice.

While I was grateful for Brandon's transparency, it wasn't until years later, after we divorced and I finally felt ready to date again, that I started to come to terms with what it was like to be living with herpes. I felt immense dread in having to share this precious information with men who may or may not be around in a few months. So I kept things light and casual and tried to avoid sexual contact with men, even if I really liked them.

That all changed when I was introduced to Dr. Boyd. From our very first session, she always made me feel safe, cared for, and that there was nothing I could do to make me unlovable. Dr. B is an expression of God on the earth in my life. When I whimpered to her, "I have herpes," she consoled, "Oh, sweet girl! You have herpes, and that makes me love you *more*!" I was undone. I had never thought to look at the parts of myself that I considered unsavory and integrate them into the fabric of my being. Dr. B taught me how to tenderly care for my emotional and spiritual wounds. Y'all . . . *good* therapy is like a great orgasm: explosive, satisfying, life-changing, and it keeps you coming back for more. Please don't let your community shame you into thinking that "therapy is for white people," or that if you go to therapy you must be "crazy."* Remember, you are worthy of holistic, abundant care, and therapy is your birthright!

In fact, I have free mental healthcare for African-descended people as a line item in Lyvonne's Reparations Package. In my drafted memo to the United States, I list a plethora of services and products that would begin to recompense the descendants of enslaved Africans for the residual effects of slavery, racism, colonialism, domestic terrorism, and anti-Blackness.

---

* We need to release using the word "crazy" because it is an offensive term. It is ableist language and harmful to use in the context of mental healthcare.

I demand:

- Student loan debt forgiveness and reimbursement
- Mortgage forgiveness and reimbursement
- Free college tuition to any institution
- A single family home situated on one acre of land
- Free mental healthcare
- An International Day of Mourning (a paid-time-off day for members of the African Diaspora to grieve the atrocities our people have suffered)
- Transferring ownership of visual and recorded art to the heirs of the original creators
- Returning artifacts that have been hijacked for museums to the rightful tribal owners
- Compensation to the descendants of famed artists who had their work stolen, copied, or plagiarized by successful white artists (think Elvis Presley's wealth being transferred to Sammy Davis, Jr.'s descendants)
- Free African Ancestry DNA testing so we know which tribes we come from
- An all-expenses-paid birthright trip to the villages we came from to meet our tribal families

I'm sure I will add to this list over time, but all of these efforts would be preliminary steps to restoring the physical, mental, financial, and spiritual well-being of Black folks on this land. Our inheritance, in the form of reparations, can and should be robust and holistic.

....

There's Nothing Prodigal About You

In the parable of the prodigal son[2] we encounter two sons, one who demands his inheritance early and goes out and squanders it, and the other who stays dutifully by his father's side. When the son who left has run out of money, he returns home only to be welcomed and celebrated by his father. The son who stayed is, rightfully so, pissed that his seemingly irresponsible brother got to go live it up and party while he stayed behind and worked hard for years. The brother who stayed refused to honor the brother who returned. From this passage we are to believe that the moral of the story is: Be happy for the reunion and God will forgive us for straying.

But what about those of us who left home because home wasn't safe? The ones who stayed even when people called us "stupid" and anything BUT a child of God. What about those of us who are parenting as best we can, trying to create new generational patterns not steeped in codependency and dysfunction? Chile, this story is about so much more than spending money frivolously—it is a mirror of what it feels like to be unconditionally loved and supported. The gospel (the actual good news!) is that there is NOTHING you can do that will make you unlovable. On your worst day, with your worst attitude and your suckiest energy, you are *still* worthy of tenderness, compassion, and care.

Coming home to my body has meant learning to welcome, embrace, and cherish the parts of myself that I've been socialized to believe are distasteful. There is nothing nasty about my body. I let that refrain soak into my being and lavished myself with adoration and, after a time of celibacy, I started to reengage with men. I even had a magical one-night stand with this 6′5″, dark-skinned, successful educator with a megawatt smile who, while we were smoking a joint, confessed to me that he had seen my most recent Instagram post. I had shared that I had contracted genital herpes, both as a way to destigmatize the condition and to let people interested in my spiritual life-coaching services know that there was NOTHING off topic for us to explore.

"You know, what you posted about? How do you talk about that?" he hesitantly broached.

"What?" I knew *exactly* what he was referring to, but I wanted to hear him say the words.

"What you posted about . . . I have that, too. How do you bring that up?"

We basically had the conversation without having the conversation and I was reminded, once again, that these growing pains about our sexuality transcend gender. It also let me know that I was on the right path, because that night we had some AMAZING sex. Like, phenomenal.

But I digress.

I know it's intimidating, beloved, but I encourage you to take the leap and share (with important people who matter; not the asshole who ghosts you after one date . . . use your discernment!). Because, y'all! Out of all the men I have disclosed my condition to, only one (1!) has had a concern about it. And since we were coworkers, I honestly think it was for the best that we disengaged romantically. I would even consider it divine protection since office romances can get messy so I'm gonna take it as: Transparency and I are undefeated.

Won't You Be Your Neighbor?

Every day is a beautiful day in the neighborhood when you love where you live, and I don't mean your zip code. Home is not an address. . . . Home is where you feel safe. As Black women who committed ourselves to a belief system that disserved us, it is time for us to reclaim the time that the locusts of poor theology and patriarchal oppression stole from us. It is our season to restore safety as our home frequency. If we are in any space that does not make us feel secure, it is well within our rights to leave that space and shake the dust off our feet.

Now is the time for you to unlearn any religious, social, and cultural conditioning that makes you think your body is unholy and release any insecurities you might have about your body-temple.

Inner dialogue is a major component of fostering radical self-love. How do you talk to yourself? What do you say about yourself when you look in the mirror?

What was the last thing you said to your reflection? Would you say the same thing to your five-year-old god-daughter? In her book *Self-Compassion: The Proven Power of Being Kind to Yourself,* Dr. Kristin Neff offers insight into the healthiest ways to speak to yourself. She explains that the way you would talk to your baby niece or nephew is the way you should be talking to yourself. You must treat yourself the way you treat people you love. If you wouldn't say it to a child, it should not be said to you. After all, you still have an inner child who walks with you, "the brave bruised girlchild within each of us,"[3] so when you speak kindly to your today-year-old self, you're speaking kindly to baby you, too!

Beloved, if you can't speak to yourself with kindness, this shows that you do not love yourself. While you may like yourself because of what you do, you do not truly love yourself simply because of who you are. That is an agonizing reality to sit with. But it's not your fault! Religious, social, and cultural indoctrination taught you *not* to! The hope for tomorrow is that you *can* learn to love yourself and it starts with loving your body, your sensuality, and your sexuality. Period.

And for those of you who are also living with a sexually transmitted disease or infection, beloved, know that you are worthy. You are worthy of decadent dates, sumptuous sex, oceanic orgasms, and luscious love. You must own, at a cellular level, that you are wildly worthy of the whimsical, whirlwind, ritzy romance your heart desires. Your condition is a *part* of you, but it does NOT define you!

I need you to take a deep, cleansing breath, and trust God and yourself. You know it's time to talk to him. You know it's time to tell her. The last time y'all were together, things got hot and heavy, and you panicked. You rolled from off top (or from underneath) and made up an excuse about why you had to go. You told him you just shaved and had to wait a day or two. You lied and said that your BV* is flaring up again. "It's that time of the month" or "I have a yeast infection," you evaded. My love, if you care about this person, they deserve to know. And the more you like them, the sooner you need to tell them. If they shun you for your condition, then they simply are not the one.

I know it can seem scary, but here's how I bring up the topic as part of a general sexual wellness conversation:

"When was the last time you were tested?" I present this query soon after I sense physical chemistry and well before we find ourselves in a sexual encounter. I love it because it shows that I am curious about my potential partner's responsibility for his health and wellness, and I care about us being safe should we become sexually involved.

That usually leads to a conversation on STDs. I sometimes have to ask very specifically, "What have you ever tested positive for?" because, remember, men also suffer from the same social stigma and societal shame. When it's my turn to share, I reveal my status (it is the only way to be ethical, Sis) and say something like, "I contracted genital herpes from a former partner. I don't have outbreaks often and, when I do,

---

* Bacterial vaginosis is a common condition of bacterial overgrowth in the vagina that can cause itching, discharge, and unpleasant odors.

I manage them." The next question is usually "Well, are you good *now?*" And we proceed to have AMAZING consensual, (usually) protected sex. After my initial herpes diagnosis, I had made up this whole narrative in my head that I would never have sex or find love again. False. Lies. Deceit. Y'all . . . *trust* me. I'm sexing and I'm sexing GOODT.

I'm not telling you what I think—I'm telling you what I know. I couldn't even finish writing this book until I came home to myself. I had to go through **years** of unlearning and relearning, crying and wailing, grieving and raging, releasing and purging to get to a place where I could have sex with a man I love without rolling over and crying. Or have sex with a man I *don't* love, but with whom I was able to share in a magical, mystical, meaningful experience. Every pleasurable, sexy moment of my life is like a bulb on a string of lights, illuminating my path to agency and wholeness.

God Doesn't Care About Who You're Sleeping With

Some of the most unkind thoughts I've had about myself relate to how dangerously dependent God's love for me is based upon my sexual inactivity. In fact, I spent almost a decade priding myself on the fact that I was celibate and, therefore, "more holy." Due to toxic programming, we've been made to believe that we should shame ourselves for engaging in sexual acts. Think of all the days, weeks, years, *decades* you've spent agonizing over whether or not your being sexually active is the reason why God blocked your promotion at work. Or believing that your financial troubles were caused not by a gendered, racialized pay gap but because you engaged in pleasurable, ethical, consensual sex. Do you see how twisted this is? You're not a pretzel. It's time to unravel yourself, Sis.

There is no way to contort your natural makeup to fit

some unrealistic veneer of "holiness." You are holy because God is holy and, like my friend Tina Lifford proclaimed, "God don't make no mess!" Tina had emblazoned this powerful affirmation on a poster with her bright-smiled face at her Inner Fitness | Outer Beauty Tour stop in Atlanta and it resonated so deeply with me.

Your body is holy, Sis. Just as it is. You cannot live your best life now if you are constantly at war with your body. The relationship you inherited with your flesh is complicated; I get that. But, like that annoying knot in your favorite lariat necklace, it is up to you to pause, sit, and take the time, energy, and diligence to detangle the snags in your psyche. This is your divine call to continue to foster self-compassion and self-acceptance on your self-love journey!

Heeding the Call to Return Home

There is no way you can get to self-love without first accepting *all* of who you are, and you will never accept all of who you are if you don't first have compassion for yourself. Be gracious with yourself. Be kind. Curate your social media timeline in such a way that you are fed and full once you close out the app. Follow Black women healers' accounts that proffer uncensored, culturally relevant content. Unfollow anyone who broadcasts Black death, makes you roll your eyes, makes you feel "ugh," or doesn't make you feel good about yourself. And don't be afraid to unplug. FOMO (Fear of Missing Out) is an illusion. Listening to what your spirit needs *is* listening to your body! Consistently listen to her and you will NEVER miss out on anything that's for you!

Hear me: What's for you will not miss you.

That's why you get to say where and when you heal. Your woundedness is not your fault, but it is your responsibility to heal. We must begin, or deepen, our healing journeys in order to live the abundant life that Jesus and Scripture promise us. We must honor the totality of who we are, as human beings with feelings and flesh. We must not despise these holy entities, because feelings and flesh are our sacred texts and sensuality is our spiritual practice.

> Embrace new descriptors for God: Healer, Designer, Provider, Creator, Father/Mother, Parent, whatever makes you feel sweet, held, loved, and adored—because you are.

Changing our language about God will change our view of God. See God as the loving, kind, healing source of energy that God is. Embrace new descriptors for God: Healer, Designer, Provider, Creator, Father/Mother, Parent, whatever makes you feel sweet, held, loved, and adored—because you are. If you continue to think that the God who made you hates you, you will never see God in your flesh, and you will never *love* that flesh. Don't be so concerned with what to call God that you don't see God, especially when you look in the mirror.

Swing into Your Power

In December 2018, I went to Bali for a yoga and manifestation retreat for Black women. During one of our fabulous excursions, we went to Bali Swing theme park, an adrenaline junkie's paradise. Situated in the lush jungle, there were four different swings, ranging in height from 32 to 255 feet tall. Imagine soaring high above trees, rice fields, rivers, canyons, and cliffs as you glide back and forth through the tropical landscape. The views were Insta-worthy for sure!

I was standing in line and kiki'ing with Lauren Ash, a meditation and wellness expert and the founder of Black

Girl in Om, when I mentioned that I was excited about the big swing, but I wanted try this "baby one" first.

"You know this *is* the big swing, right?" Lauren asked quizzically.

"It is?" I had thought it was the short one.

"Do people tell you that you make hard things look easy?" Lauren sweetly inquired.

Her question didn't need any time to hang in the thick, sweet Indonesian air, because it immediately resonated deeply with me. I nodded knowingly. "Yeah."

The tallest swing, which floated 255 feet in the air, looked like a practice run to me! This realization of my power and affirmation of my capacity were like palm-tree-shaped hugs from God.

God purposed and enabled me to make hard things look easy, but that doesn't mean that the trials and tribulations I have experienced in my lifetime were any less difficult. It just means I need (and continuously offer myself) that much more grace, kindness, compassion, and intentionality to continue healing, evolving, and expanding.

When it was my turn, I stepped toward the swing attendants, who strapped me into a harness and asked me if I was ready. I smiled brightly and told them I was. They held the swing steady as I took my seat, my flowy floral dress already floating around my ankles from a beautiful Balinese breeze. The attendants yelled the affirmations for me to keep my hands high on the ropes and my feet off the ground. When they pushed the swing, I felt an exhilarating rush of energy. Like I could fly . . . like I *was* flying.

I was also hollering! But it was an invigorating, once-in-a-lifetime opportunity that I would do again in a heartbeat.

That's the truth of my life journey, y'all. You've read through some of the major valleys in my life. And that's just what would fit in *this* book! But for all the joys and pains, I wouldn't change a thing. I would not be the person I am today had I not gone through the things I went through. I'm not saying that God needed me to suffer so that she would be glorified. But I do know that I needed God through it all. And, it's because of God that I've pirouetted on peaks and now celebrate life as a sexually liberated Black woman of faith.

My wounds became scars and my pain transformed into my medicine. Today, I am able to offer my wisdom to a wounded world. And what helps me fulfill my purpose is the continued healing I receive through telling the truth. The truth is hard to say and sometimes harder to hear, but God is willing to bear the burden with us.

As such, I consider myself the queen of hard topics; the word "taboo" isn't even in my lexicon. I tell my story because it is *never* just MY story. People always mention how "strong" and "courageous" I am for sharing so openly. While I am honored to be seen as brave, vulnerability is my superpower. And it is not unique to me. In fact, vulnerability is a trait that can be fostered in all of us. In order to nurture openness among us, we must normalize speaking and hearing the truth, even (especially!) when it's hard. When asked, "How are you?" rather than a flippant "fine" or an automatic "good," I would love for us to say we're hurting, we're struggling, we're sad, or simply, "I'm having a tough day—are you in a space to listen?"

We can do this, y'all. We can have hard conversations. We can be brave. We've already seen it fully lived and expressed in the historical Christ figure. Jesus walked the earth calling out oppressive powers and hypocritical leaders, beckoning us to love God and neighbor. But you cannot say that you love God if you do not love yourself. You cannot love your neighbor without loving yourself first. "Self-love is the absolute first step to loving others."[4]

The love and liberation of Black folks depend on the love and liberation of self. You cannot holler "Black Lives Matter!" and not believe that your body matters, too. "Our bodies are the vessels of God's abiding love. To be able to love our own bodies is to be able to accept God's love of us."[5] God cares about your body, beloved. And what happens to your body matters.

Body Matters

During my time in Bali, I learned about the Japanese art of *kintsugi. Kintsugi,* meaning "golden seams," is the art of repairing broken pottery. And not in the DIY-home-project way; rather, in the restoring-of-what's-in-need-of-mending way. The origin story goes that Ashikaga Yoshimasa, a fifteenth-century shogun,* broke his favorite Chinese tea bowl. He sent it back to China to be repaired but was displeased with the metal they used for the seams. Yoshimasa, ever persistent, decided to entrust Japanese artisans with the delicate task of restoring his precious possession.

> WE GET TO BE BOTH WORKS OF ART AND WORKS IN PROGRESS AT THE SAME DAMN TIME!

The Japanese craftsmen, expert creatives and well-versed in aesthetics, blended gold powder with lacquered resin and used this metallic mixture to fill the cracks of the tea bowl. Yoshimasa was so thrilled with the result that he proudly dis-

---

* "Shogun" means "heavenly sovereign" and is a Japanese "chief priest" or military leader.

played it in his home. Visitors would always comment on how beautiful it was and he was typically happy to relay the story behind the unique piece.

Just as our lives are living epistles, our bodies are works of art. We are living, breathing *kintsugi* pieces, bearing about in our bodies the parts of ourselves that were wounded but not irreparable. If we would lay the chipped pieces of our low self-esteem, dissociation with our bodies, and disconnection with our sexuality before God, the Creator will fill our cracks with golden light and healing love. *Kintsugi* teaches us that any harm we have suffered is not meant to be discarded, but rather brought out into the light and mended so that what remains is a beautiful divine design. And the most luscious part is that we get to be both works of art and works in progress at the same damn time!

Our resiliency is admirable, yes, but I long for a time when Black women can cease to be resilient and commence being at ease. In my highest imagination,* we don't need to be strong; we thrive by being soft. We don't have to be tough; we welcome being tender. We don't gotta be durable; we get to be dainty.

As we unfold to softness, our radical self-acceptance will bloom. There are so many beautiful opportunities for growth and healing waiting for us on the journey. The invitation you've been longing for is here. The confirmation you've been praying for has arrived. The permission you've been desiring has been granted.

Scripture declares that "if two of you agree on earth about anything you ask, it will be done for you."[6] That's me and you, Sis. Additionally, Jesus professed that "where two or three are gathered in my name, I am there among them."[7] You are not alone. We are in this together. There are others

---

* I first head this language from EbonyJanice Moore.

who think, feel, and ponder like you do. Take a few moments to make a list of people you feel safe enough around to start these holistic conversations. Now read your list aloud. This list is now a prayer request. Trust God that you are divinely aligned and on the right path, and ask for the wisdom to nurture those relationships.

You can love God *and* love sex. In fact, loving your mind, body, and spirit, your FULL self, *is* loving God. After all, you are an expression of the Divine in human flesh. We were fooled into thinking that our bodies are somehow separate from our spirits and never the two shall meet. Darling ones, we get to break the molds we were given and start new traditions that help our interior dialogue resound with thoughts of love and care. If you truly want to live the most abundant, lavish life that God wills for you, you must embody the understanding that:

God loves you.
You are an expression of the Divine.
Your ancestors are riding for you.
Your community has your front, back, and sides.

Honestly assess: Where do you find your community? You can always start at home. Honoring and maintaining what brings you joy is the best, most honest way to create community with yourself. What is your relationship to your ancestors like? Do you have one? If you've been waiting for permission to connect with your ancestors, this is it! If you're looking for a Black Christian–adjacent, African-centered worship space, tap in with these spiritual gatherings to nourish your soul and glean inspiration for our spiritual journeys: Sensual Faith Sunday and The Proverbial Experience (led by me), Pink Robe Chronicles (curated by Rev. Dr. Melva Sampson), The Gathering: A Womanist Church (co-pastored by Rev. Dr. Irie Lynne

Session and Rev. Kamilah Hall Sharp), and other Black women–led digital spaces that engage in deep reflection of our faith and interrogation of our sacred texts.

You are worthy of love, joy, money, wealth, GREAT sex, orgasms, pleasure, ease, flow, and *Surthrival*. You don't have to do, be, or say anything to be worthy. You are inherently worthy because you are a child of God. So remind yourself of that every day. And, one day in the near or distant future, you will look in the mirror and profess:

Welcome HOME.

There will be no application process. You were born certified. There is no minimum credit score required. You were born approved. There is no need for a cosigner. You were born authorized. There is no housing association. You were born endorsed. You are privileged to adorn your home any way *you* choose, so why not make it lovely? Surround yourself with beauty. Buy yourself fresh flowers. Burn intoxicating incense. Only wear clothing that makes you feel regal or like a baddie.

Danyiel Wright, a home healing and decor coach and interior designer, says: "Heal your home, design your life." Curating a beautiful home is not just about aesthetics, although my astrological and spiritual backgrounds confirm that visual stimuli are a way of life for me. Surrounding yourself with beauty reminds you that you, too, are beautiful. A picturesque home space amplifies that you are a precious, sacred object, and you should be treated as such in *every* area of your life!

So, as you drape new window treatments, wipe off the window to your soul. As you arrange a lush bouquet of roses, remind yourself to rise in your power. As you hang framed Black art, be sure to fangirl over your own frame. Your body is not only your home—it is your sanctuary. Your spirit should be so fortified that whenever you feel like the outside world is unkind, you have an interior world so large, so wondrous, so hospitable, that you can baptize yourself in affection. Will there be moments when you need someone else to submerge you in lavish love? Absolutely. But by and large, Sis, you have the capacity to do this yourself. This is your strength and superpower. Yes, God's strength is made perfect in our weakness, and as Ntozake Shange says, "i found god in myself & i loved her / i loved her fiercely."[8]

When I accepted the truth about God, I accepted the truth about myself. Once I honored the reality of the Divine, I honored the divinity within myself. The Creator is not lacking in anything, and neither am I. I am a divine being of light here to evolve the earth. I am holy. I am a sacred expression of Source, and so are you. And since God created us with the natural capacity to experience sexual pleasure, then sexual pleasure must be our birthright.

Remember, our sexuality is not separate from who we are. It is a part of us, and we are good. Just as we are. Embrace yourself wholly and remind yourself that you are holy. God has the perfect home for you, and guess what? You're already in it. Even if you desire a few renovations, you are already where you need to be. Otherwise, you would be somewhere else. Where you are right now is serving you, so go ahead and place your hand on the handle of truth. Unlock the bolt to your body, swing your sensuality wide open, step into your power, and decadently declare . . .

It's good to be home.

Reflect:

Very truly, I tell you, the one who believes in me will also do the works that I do and, in fact, will do greater works than these. . . . (John 14:12)

Celebrate:

What about you makes you love yourself more fiercely? If you need help thinking through this, write down a list of all the things that you don't like about yourself: the things you wish you could change, often say unkind things about, or conveniently left *out* of your Instagram bio. And now, after reading each of those things, add on, "and that makes me love you more." Watch what happens over the course of days and weeks as you integrate the parts of yourself that you deemed unlovable to become not just loved but affirmed and celebrated!

Affirm:

My body is holy—just as it is.
God is good and so is my body.
I am loved.

Acknowledgments

Whew, chile! We made it. Lissen. God, I THANK YOU! There are SO many moments that led to this one and I'm gonna savor it. Because I am HERE, baby! And it's by the grace of GOD.

I would be remiss if I didn't start out by thanking her (like I'm a hip-hop star at an awards show, LOL!). No, but, forreal. To my God. My Creator. My Source, I give thanks.

To my ancestors, you are my bones, my shelter, and my hiding place. Thank you for loving me the way that you do. To Nana Norma, Grandpa Eric, Aunty Paula, Robert Briggs, A. Knighton Stanley, Fannie Lou Hamer, and my great cloud of witnesses, I see you, I honor you, I love you. *Aṣe.*

To my spiritual cabinet, the Orishas, especially Oshun

and Shango, my angels, spirit guides, and deities. I am honored to be your child.

To the motherlands that hold me: New York, New Orleans, Atlanta, Oakland, Sierra Leone, Angola, Barbados, and Guyana, I give thanks.

If I start calling names, I'mma forget someone, so I'm not even going to try. To my family, biological, spiritual, or otherwise: I adore you. To my mom, Merlene, thank you for birthing me and instilling church in me. Your "I don't care what you do on Saturday night, as long as you in church on Sunday morning" landed well, LOL! To my nephew Mason, may the best of me dwell in you.

To my pastors, who always affirmed what God was doing in and through me, especially Rev. Dr. Maisha Kariamu Handy and Rize Community Church, Rev. Dr. Melva Sampson and the Pink Robe Chronicles family, and Pastor Michael McBride and The Way Christian Center. To my Caribbean kin who nurtured me and my ministry when I was a little girl at St. James the Less Episcopal Church in Queens, to catching the Holy Ghost at Holiness Pentecostal Church of Christ in Newark, New Jersey, to serving at Community Baptist Church in New Haven. To the congregations that called me "Pastor": St. Paul's Community Baptist Church in Philadelphia and Friendship Missionary Baptist Church in Vallejo, California.

To the leadership of The Proverbial Experience, Proverbial Kin, and the entire Sensual Faith tribe—thank you for trusting and loving me.

To Mrs. Zimmermann, my third-grade teacher. When I wrote and read aloud my short story about a raven in a tree (and this was WAY before I knew about Edgar Allan Poe), you announced triumphantly to me, in front of the entire class, "Lyvonne, you can be a writer when you grow up." Look how I've grown!

To Ms. McKay, my tenth-grade English teacher. You introduced me to Sula, a woman with body, agency, and a will to live, love, and THRIVE. You also made space for me to play and take risks with poetry and prose, and today, I, like Sula, am a literary baddie!

To my beloved professors and colleagues at Yale Divinity School and Columbia Theological Seminary, thank you for igniting my theological imagination. To my Forum for Theological Exploration (FTE), DO GOOD X, and Auburn Seminary mentors and co-conspirators—thank you for giving me space to play, dream, and grow.

Candice Benbow, I am so inspired by you! From being a fan of your work in seminary to becoming your labelmate—you have shown up for me in ways known and unknown, in ways seen and yet to be seen. It only took us a decade to meet! LOLOL! Thank you.

Deep thanks to my author comrades Terence Lester, Jennifer Harvey, Linda Kay Klein, Rose Gwynn, Rabbi Rebekah Stern, and Tina Lifford. I so appreciate your guidance.

To Liz Kineke, who catalyzed these shenanigans, thank you for championing me and my work.

Rachelle Gardner, thank you for catching the vision. You are not just my literary agent, you are my friend. Thank you for being a champion and a cheerleader.

To Tina Constable, Convergent Books, and Penguin Random House, from editors to sales and marketing, from the roota to the toota, thank you for walking alongside me, believing in my dream, and amplifying my work. It's the good trouble for me!

To Becky Nesbitt, for learning from and with me and caring for me beyond my work. To Porscha Burke, for being my first reflection and affirmation (and the powerhouse who was the last person to edit Dr. Maya Angelou's work!), I thank you. God knew we needed to create a holy trinity of editorial goodness and, because of y'all, I sound even sharper, clearer, and more profound . . . how that sound? *cartwheel*

To my therapist, Dr. Briana Boyd. We are God. I love you.

To my Sisters—Juju, EbonyJanice, Danielle, Danyiel, Danyelle, and Phoenix, thank you for holding me toward the sun. To my Fam Bam, Sawrahs, Sunflower Sisters, and Caribbean gyals the world over, much love.

To Shaun, Marcell, Jeremy, Romal, Mahlik, and BBMR, thank you for showing me what it means to be loved well by Black men.

For everyone who is a part of my community, my tribe, and my village, you know who you are and I am so grateful that I get to share time and space with you. Thank you for loving me tew gud!

And, lastly, shout-out to me! I am so proud of you, Lyvonne, for doing your work, healing, evolving, and sharing your gifts with the world. Now whine up ya waist and walk fully into your destiny.

God's fingerprint on my life is always this one door swung wide open for me. I am grateful for that kind of care. A care we all deserve. We are all so very, very *worthy*.

Go in peace, go in power, go in pleasure. Be well, beloved ones. And if it's not well . . . it's not the end!

With deep gratitude,
Lyvonne

Resources

If you're struggling or having a hard time right now, there's 24/7 support, Sis.

988 Suicide & Crisis Lifeline (formerly the National Suicide Hotline)
988 or 800-273-8255

Crisis Text Line
Text HOME to 741741

Therapy Options

Open Path Psychotherapy Collective
Offers lower-cost therapy for people of color.
openpathcollective.org

Loveland Foundation

Founded by public intellectual Rachel Cargle. They subsidize therapy costs for Black women. thelovelandfoundation.org/therapy-fund

Talkspace

An easy-peasy option for beginning talk therapy. talkspace.com

Notes

Author's Note

1. Genesis 1:31.

Chapter 1: Aching for Home:
Learning to Ease Spiritual Homesickness

1. 1 Corinthians 6:19 (King James Version).
2. See Rev. Dr. Mack King Carter, excerpt from the sermon "Why America Rejects the Biblical Christ" (text: 1 Cor. 1:18, 22–24). Delivered October 5, 1987, in the Martin Lu-

ther King Jr. International Chapel at Morehouse College, Atlanta.

3. Kelly Brown Douglas, *Sexuality and the Black Church: A Womanist Perspective* (Maryknoll, NY: Orbis Books, 1999), 123.

4. Toni Morrison, *Beloved* (New York: Vintage International, 2019), 103.

5. Alice Walker, *In Search of Our Mothers' Gardens: Womanist Prose* (New York: A Harvest Book, 2004), xi–xii.

6. "Alabama Senate Election Results," *The Washington Post,* December 12, 2017, https://www.washingtonpost.com /special-election-results/alabama/.

7. "An Examination of the 2016 Electorate, Based on Validated Voters," Pew Research Center, August 9, 2018, https://www.pewresearch.org/politics/2018/08/09/an -examination-of-the-2016-electorate-based-on-validated -voters/.

8. Ruth Igielnik, Scott Keeter, and Hannah Hartig, "Behind Biden's 2020 Victory: An Examination of the 2020 Electorate, Based on Validated Voters," Pew Research Center, June 30, 2021, https://www.pewresearch.org/politics/2021/06 /30/behind-bidens-2020-victory/.

9. Genesis 1:28.

10. *Nina Simone: A Historical Perspective,* directed by Peter Rodis (1970), Dailymotion, 14:13–15:43, https://www.dailymotion .com/video/x14hgds.

11. Brown Douglas, *Sexuality and the Black Church,* 123.

Chapter 2: "Body" Is Not a Four-Letter Word:
Renewing Your Mind About Your Flesh

1. Kate Pickles, "Do YOU Know Your Vulva from Your Vagina? Half of Women Can't Identify Their Reproductive Parts on a Diagram," *Daily Mail,* September 2, 2016,

https://www.dailymail.co.uk/health/article-3771189/Do
-know-vulva-vagina-Half-women-t-identify-reproductive
-parts-diagram.html.

2. GirlTrek, "Angela Davis and Nikki Giovanni's LIVE Discussion with GirlTrek," YouTube, May 9, 2020, panel interview, 1:21:03–1:21:12, https://www.youtube.com/watch?v
=esPHDvx_aZc&t=2288s.

3. Job 2:9 (Easy-to-Read Version).

4. Brown Douglas, *Sexuality and the Black Church,* 123.

5. Zahra Mulroy, "Doctors Finally Confirm Period Pain Can Be as Painful as a Heart Attack and Women Are Rejoicing," *Mirror,* March 6, 2018, https://www.mirror.co.uk
/lifestyle/health/doctors-finally-confirm-your-period
-12103914.

6. Delores S. Williams, *Sisters in the Wilderness: The Challenge of Womanist God-Talk* (Maryknoll, NY: Orbis, 1995), 67.

7. Katie Geneva Cannon, *Katie's Canon: Womanism and the Soul of the Black Community, Revised and Expanded 25th Anniversary Edition* (Minneapolis: Fortress Press, 2021), 35.

Chapter 3: "I Had a Feeling":
Trusting Your Gut and Nurturing Your Intuition

1. Joy DeGruy, *Post Traumatic Slave Syndrome: America's Legacy of Enduring Injury and Healing* (Portland, OR: Joy DeGruy Publications, 2017), 105.

2. Ibid., 25.

3. Goddess Lulabelle, "FLORIDA WATER for Cleansing and Clearing," YouTube, August 17, 2017, 4:00–4:03, https://
www.youtube.com/watch?v=Xeo2cvlPubc.

4. Clarissa Pinkola Estés, PhD, *Women Who Run with the Wolves: Myths and Stories of the Wild Woman Archetype* (New York: Ballantine Books, 1997), 117.

5. Georgetown Law's Center on Poverty and Inequality, "Research Confirms That Black Girls Feel the Sting of Adultification Bias Identified in Earlier Georgetown Law Study," Georgetown Law, May 15, 2019, https://www.law.george town.edu/news/research-confirms-that-black-girls-feel-the -sting-of-adultification-bias-identified-in-earlier-georgetown -law-study/.

6. Psalm 51:5 (KJV).

7. Nadine Burke Harris, *The Deepest Well: Healing the Long-Term Effects of Childhood Adversity* (New York: Houghton Mifflin Harcourt, 2018), 98.

8. Estés, *Women Who Run with the Wolves*, 111.

9. Rev. Dr. Wil Gafney, "Translation Matters: A Fem/Womanist Exploration of Translation Theory and Practice for Proclamation in Worship," The Society of Biblical Literature, https://www.sbl-site.org/assets/pdfs/gafney.pdf.

Chapter 4: "But the Bible Says . . .":
Acknowledging What Church and Society Got Wrong

1. Song of Songs 1:2.

2. Song of Songs 1:4.

3. Nathaniel Samuel Murrell, "Song of Songs," from Crystal Downing and Rodney S. Sadler, Jr., eds., *The Africana Bible: Reading Israel's Scriptures from Africa and the African Diaspora* (Minneapolis: Fortress Press, 2009), 255–59.

4. Jennifer Wright Knust, *Unprotected Texts: The Bible's Surprising Contradictions About Sex and Desire* (New York: HarperCollins, 2012), 23–24.

5. Stacey M. Floyd-Thomas, ed., *Deeper Shades of Purple: Womanism in Religion and Society* (New York: New York University Press, 2006).

6. Philip Goff, Arthur E. Farnsley II, and Peter J. Thuesen, eds., *The Bible in American Life* (New York: Oxford University Press, 2017), 10.

7. Ibid., 8.

8. Randall C. Bailey, Tat-siong Benny Liew, and Fernando F. Segovia, eds., *They Were All Together in One Place? Toward Minority Biblical Criticism* (Atlanta: Society of Biblical Literature, 2009), 234–35.

9. Frederic W. Bush, *World Biblical Commentary: Ruth-Esther, Volume 9* (Grand Rapids, MI: Zondervan, 2018), 153.

10. Ibid.

11. Knust, *Unprotected Texts,* 5.

12. Karen Baker-Fletcher and Garth Kasimu Baker-Fletcher, *My Sister, My Brother: Womanist and Xodus God-Talk* (New York: Orbis Books, 1997), 26.

13. Juju Bae, "N*ggas Die Different," A Little Juju Podcast, April 21, 2020, Podcast Episode 45, 25:09–25:32, https://soundcloud.com/user-991694293/ep-45-n-ggas-die-different.

14. Hebrews 12:1.

15. Matthew 17:1–8, Mark 9:2–8, and Luke 9:28–36.

16. For one such example see Jonathan Vroom, "Recasting Mišpāṭîm: Legal Innovation in Leviticus 24:10–23," *Journal of Biblical Literature* 131, no. 1 (April 2012): 27–44, https://doi.org/10.2307/23488210.

17. Gafney, 3.

18. 1 Peter 2:4–5, 9.

19. 2 Corinthians 3:17.

20. Joshua Harris, "'I Kissed Dating Goodbye' Author: How and Why I've Rethought Dating and Purity Culture," *USA Today,* November 23, 2018, https://www.usatoday.com/story/opinion/voices/2018/11/23/christianity-kissed-dating-goodbye-relationships-sex-book-column/2071273002/.

Chapter 5: #MeToo, Sis:
Healing Sexual Trauma and Fostering Resiliency

1. Rape, Abuse & Incest National Network, https://www
   .rainn.org/statistics.
2. Catherine Townsend, "Estimating a Child Sexual Abuse
   Prevalence Rate for Practitioners: A Review of Child Sexual
   Abuse Prevalence Studies," Darkness to Light, August
   2013, 21, https://www.d2l.org/wp-content/uploads/2017
   /02/PREVALENCE-RATE-WHITE-PAPER-D2L.pdf.
3. Tiffany Thomas, "The Legacy of Women in the Black
   Church," *Christianity Today,* February 11, 2016, https://www
   .christianitytoday.com/women-leaders/2016/february
   /legacy-of-women-in-black-church.html?paging=off.
4. Megachurch Hillsong, founded and globally pastored by
   Brian Houston, has been riddled with sexual abuse scandals,
   including the alleged cover-up of his father's sexual abuse
   of children. For more, see Hannah Ritchie, "Australian
   Megachurch Founder Steps Down Amid Allegations of
   Misconduct," CNN, March 23, 2022, https://www.cnn.com
   /2022/03/23/australia/australia-megachurch-founder
   -misconduct-allegations-intl/index.html.
5. Tamura Lomax, *Jezebel Unhinged: Loosing the Black Female Body
   in Religion and Culture* (Durham, NC: Duke University Press,
   2018), 32.
6. Cameron Kimble, "Sexual Assault Remains Dramatically
   Underreported," Brennan Center for Justice, October 4,
   2018, https://www.brennancenter.org/our-work/analysis
   -opinion/sexual-assault-remains-dramatically
   -underreported.
7. Conor Friedersdorf, "The Understudied Female Sexual
   Predator," *The Atlantic,* November 28, 2016, https://www

.theatlantic.com/science/archive/2016/11/the
-understudied-female-sexual-predator/503492/.

8. The Black Church Center for Justice and Equality. "#Black-ChurchAgenda (Sexual Violence in Church and Society)," YouTube, January 19, 2019, 26:00–28:48, https://www.youtube.com/watch?v=U0td_87PyJM.

9. Lomax, *Jezebel Unhinged,* 205.

10. Phyllis Trible, *Texts of Terror: Literary-Feminist Readings of Biblical Narratives* (Philadelphia: Fortress Press, 1984).

11. Strong's Concordance lists "seized" as one of the translations of the Hebrew word. See Strong's Concordance, "lāqaḥ," Blue Letter Bible, https://www.blueletterbible.org/lexicon/h3947/kjv/wlc/0-1/.

12. Psalm 23:4 (KJV).

13. 1 Corinthians 14:34.

14. Revelation 12:11.

Chapter 6: Feel the Feels:
Honoring Your Body's Truth

1. Sobonfu Somé, *The Spirit of Intimacy: Ancient Teachings in the Ways of Relationships* (New York: William Morrow, 1999), 126–27.

2. Christine C. Greves, MD, "Pregnancy Loss 1:4," Winnie Palmer Hospital for Women and Babies, October 30, 2018, https://www.winniepalmerhospital.com/content-hub/pregnancy-loss-1-in-4.

3. James Baldwin, "As Much Truth as One Can Bear: To Speak Out About the World as It Is, Says James Baldwin, Is the Writer's Job," *The New York Times,* January 14, 1962, http://tweetsofanativeson.com/pdf/As-Much-Truth-As-One-Can-Bear.pdf.

4. https://www.goodreads.com/quotes/9657488-grief-i-ve
-learned-is-really-just-love-it-s-all-the.

5. "Somatic Therapy," *Psychology Today,* https://www.psychol
ogytoday.com/us/therapy-types/somatic-therapy.

6. Psalm 30:5.

Chapter 7: Pleasure Is Your Birthright:
Curating a Lavish Life of Flow and Ease

1. Nikki Katz, "Black Women Are the Most Educated Group
in the U.S.," ThoughtCo., https://www.thoughtco.com
/black-women-most-educated-group-us-4048763.

2. "The 2019 State of Women-Owned Businesses Report,"
American Express, 5, https://s1.q4cdn.com/692158879
/files/doc_library/file/2019-state-of-women-owned
-businesses-report.pdf.

3. Mathilde Roux, "5 Facts About Black Women in the Labor
Force," U.S. Department of Labor Blog, August 3, 2021,
https://blog.dol.gov/2021/08/03/5-facts-about-black
-women-in-the-labor-force.

4. Victoria M. Massie, "Black Women Are the Fastest-
Growing Group of Entrepreneurs. So Where Are the In-
vestors?," *Vox,* May 7, 2016, https://www.vox.com/2016
/3/14/11208710/kathryn-finney-diversity-tech.

5. Sophia Kunthara, "Black Women Still Receive Just a Tiny
Fraction of VC Funding Despite 5-Year High," *Crunchbase
News,* July 16, 2021, https://news.crunchbase.com/news
/something-ventured-black-women-founders/.

6. Erin L.P. Bradley, Austin M. Williams, Shana Green, et al.,
"Disparities in Incidence of Human Immunodeficiency
Virus Infection Among Black and White Women—United
States, 2010–2016," Centers for Disease Control and Pre-

vention, May 10, 2019, https://www.cdc.gov/mmwr
/volumes/68/wr/mm6818a3.htm?s_cid=mm6818a3_w.

7. "Heart Disease in African American Women," American
Heart Association, https://www.goredforwomen.org/en
/about-heart-disease-in-women/facts/heart-disease-in
-african-american-women.

8. "African American Women & Breast Cancer," Breast Cancer Prevention Partners, October 24, 2018, https://www
.bcpp.org/wp-content/uploads/2018/11/BCPP_African
-American-Women-and-Breast-Cancer_10_24_2018.pdf.

9. Elizabeth A. Stewart, Wanda K. Nicholson, Linda Bradley,
and Bijan J. Borah, "The Burden of Uterine Fibroids for
African-American Women: Results of a National Survey,"
Journal of Women's Health 22 (10): 807–816 (September 30,
2013), https://doi:10.1089/jwh.2013.4334.

10. W. McNabb, M. Quinn, and J. Tobian, "Diabetes in African
American Women: The Silent Epidemic," *Women's Health* 3
(3–4): 275–300 (September 1, 1997).

11. "Racial and Ethnic Disparities Continue in Pregnancy-
Related Deaths," Centers for Disease Control and Prevention, September 6, 2019, https://www.cdc.gov/media
/releases/2019/p0905-racial-ethnic-disparities-pregnancy
-deaths.html.

12. Joan Wylie Hall, ed., *Conversations with Audre Lorde* (Jackson:
University Press of Mississippi, 2004), 91.

13. Nina Simone penned a song, "To Be Young, Gifted, and
Black," in honor of her dear friend playwright Lorraine
Hansberry, who identified some high school visitors as
"young, gifted, and black."

14. DeGruy, *Post Traumatic Slave Syndrome: America's Legacy of Enduring Injury and Healing,* 211.

15. John 14:27.

16. "Negro Women to Be Put to Work," *The Greenville News,*

October 2, 1918, https://www.newspapers.com/clip
/38314573/negro-women-to-be-put-to-work/.

17. 1 Thessalonians 5:16–18 (The Voice).

18. John 14:12; emphasis my own.

19. Luke 1:37.

Chapter 8: Masturbation Is a Gift from God: *Getting Acquainted with Desire*

1. Paraphrase of Mark 3:25.

2. Jeremiah 17:9 (KJV).

3. 1 Corinthians 6:18 (NKJV).

4. "What Are the Parts of the Female Sexual Anatomy?,"
   Planned Parenthood, https://www.plannedparenthood.org
   /learn/health-and-wellness/sexual-and-reproductive
   -anatomy/what-are-parts-female-sexual-anatomy.

5. Ibid.

6. Matt Stefon, "Yoni," *Encyclopaedia Britannica,* https://www
   .britannica.com/topic/yoni.

7. Kristin Canning, "Yes, There Are 11 Different Types of
   Orgasms. Here's How to Have Each," *Health,* February 4,
   2020, https://www.health.com/condition/sexual-health
   /different-types-of-orgasms-0.

8. Kristine Thomason, "10 Things You Never Knew About
   the Clitoris," *Health,* October 5, 2015, https://www.health
   .com/mind-body/10-things-you-never-knew-about-the
   -clitoris.

9. Song of Songs 8:4.

10. https://www.kimbritive.com/.

11. "An Interview with Toni Cade Bambara: Kay Bonetti." In
    Thabiti Lewis, ed., *Conversations with Toni Cade Bambara* (Jackson: University Press of Mississippi, 2012), 35.

12. 1 Peter 5:8.

13. Alice Broster, "What Is the Orgasm Gap?," *Forbes,* July 31, 2020, https://www.forbes.com/sites/alicebroster/2020/07/31/what-is-the-orgasm-gap/?sh=3924b24960f8.

Chapter 9: Beautiful Scars:
Re-membering to Love Yourself Unapologetically

1. "Genital Herpes—CDC Fact Sheet (Detailed)," Center for Disease Control and Prevention, https://www.cdc.gov/std/herpes/stdfact-herpes-detailed.htm.
2. Luke 15:11–32.
3. Audre Lorde, *Sister Outsider: Essays and Speeches* (New York: Penguin Books, 2020), 169.
4. Brown Douglas, *Sexuality and the Black Church,* 123.
5. Ibid.
6. Matthew 18:19.
7. Matthew 18:20.
8. Ntozake Shange, *For Colored Girls Who Have Considered Suicide/When the Rainbow Is Enuf* (New York: Macmillan, 1977; Scribner, 2010), 63.

About the Author

Lyvonne Briggs, MDiv, ThM, an Emmy Award winner, is a body- and sex-positive womanist preacher, speaker, coach, and creator. Briggs is the host of the *Sensual Faith* podcast, co-host of the *Sanctified* podcast, and the founder of a healing-centered storytelling agency called beautiful scars, which focuses on fostering pleasure and resiliency; visionary of The Proverbial Experience; and curator of Sensual Faith Sunday, a series of virtual spiritual gatherings to nourish the soul. She has been featured in *Essence, Cosmopolitan, Rolling Stone,* and *The Washington Post,* and *Sojourners* named her one of "Eleven Women Shaping the Church." A New York City native and proud member of Delta Sigma Theta Sorority, Incorporated, Lyvonne Briggs is currently based in New Orleans, Louisiana. Follow her across platforms: @LyvonneBriggs.

About the Type

This book was set in Garamond, a typeface originally designed by the Parisian type cutter Claude Garamond (c. 1500–61). This version of Garamond was modeled on a 1592 specimen sheet from the Egenolff-Berner foundry, which was produced from types assumed to have been brought to Frankfurt by the punch cutter Jacques Sabon (c. 1536–80).

Claude Garamond's distinguished romans and italics first appeared in *Opera Ciceronis* in 1543–44. The Garamond types are clear, open, and elegant.